QUICK & EASY
INDIAN COOKING

·

Michael Pandya

Book Club Associates
London

This edition published 1983 by
Book Club Associates
By arrangement with Wm Collins Sons & Co Ltd

Copyright © Michael Pandya, 1983

Designer: Pedro Prá-Lopez
Layout: Frank Landamore
Photography: Peter Myers
Line illustrations: Barbara Wardle
Home Economist: Caroline Ellwood
Picture Stylist: Alison Williams
Cookery Editor: Barbara Croxford
Editor: Cathy Gosling

CN5188

Text set in Palatino by Rowland Phototypesetting Ltd
Bury St Edmunds, Suffolk
Colour reproduction by Intercrom S.A., Madrid, Spain
Printed and bound by
William Collins Sons & Co. Ltd.,
Glasgow

To my wife, Preeti,
and our kids Mohit, Manoj, Pawan
and Peeyush

ACKNOWLEDGEMENTS

I would like to express my gratitude to everyone who has offered me their valued comments, invaluable advice and constructive criticisms in the preparation of this book. Even after a book has been written, a lot more still has to be done before the manuscript is ready for the publisher. My wife and children have made a sterling effort towards achieving this, as they have before for my earlier books. I am obliged to them.

Thanks are also due to my sisters, Jiya and Munni, who made no mean contribution by discussing with me at great lengths various aspects of this book. My chhoti Mami, whose culinary artistry I greatly admire, has given me valuable advice and guidance – my thanks to her, too. My brother, Avadhesh, and my cousin, Birjan dada, have been instrumental in providing props and materials for the preparation of this book. Thanks to both of them.

Being a great chaat-lover, I went to the two men who have impressed me as the best chaat-makers I have known, namely, Lala and Kallu of Kanpur. They went out of their way to help me prepare the chaat section of the book. I am grateful.

My thanks to all the friendly people at Collins without whose help and cooperation this book would not have been possible.

Thanks also to the following organisations for the loan of cooking utensils and crockery for photographs, Craftsmen Potters' Shop, David Mellor, Popatal Karamashi and Sons, and Viniron Limited.

CONTENTS

INTRODUCTION

I decided to write this book in order to take up the gauntlet thrown down by those who seem to thrive on the mistaken belief that an Indian meal can never be made quickly. While I agree immediately that some main dishes do require elaborate preparation and can be time-consuming, there are literally hundreds of others which can be prepared very quickly indeed. The Indian food firmament is vast, rich and varied and caters for all tastes. If I am ultimately able to make the people of the West understand this fact, then my efforts will have been more than adequately rewarded.

This book on the 'quick and easy' aspects of Indian cookery contains carefully selected recipes, ranging from the traditional favourites: curries, pullaos, biriyanis and snacks, to the lesser known scrumptious sweetmeats, fascinating soft drinks, delicious chaat dishes and exotic chutneys, scattered throughout the book. The recipes have been adapted to suit the Western palate but without losing authenticity or taste. The book, however, aims to be more than just a collection of recipes; I hope it will pave the path to a new culinary way of life in the West! In any event, the background information, tips about the dishes, and how to present them, should further embellish your knowledge and enjoyment of Indian cookery.

But, as you can imagine, this book hardly scratches the surface of such a gigantic subject. Indian cookery is one of the oldest and most sophisticated forms of cuisine in the world, influenced by the culinary techniques of numerous nationalities that have come into contact with India over the past thousand years. In fact, no one book can boast to be an encyclopedia on the subject; it could be,

though, that with this book I may have initiated a new approach to writing on Indian cookery, as the 'quick and easy' aspect of it has hitherto largely been ignored.

Indian food is well known in the West and hardly needs an introduction; it is lovely to look at and pleases the palate. The already considerable interest in Indian food that exists in the West has been given a further stimulus by the presence of a large Indian population in many areas, which in turn has led to the opening of innumerable Indian restaurants and 'take away' places – and they all seem to be doing very good business. I am regularly asked about the 'quickies' of Indian food so I hope that this book will provide the answers.

To a Westerner, India is an inextricable part of the mysterious East. Perhaps in keeping with that image, Indian cookery tradition is surrounded by numerous explained and unexplained mysteries. It is commonly believed in India, for instance, that some cooks have 'taste' in their hands and that it rubs off on the food they cook, so that everything they cook automatically tastes delicious! Another mystery of Indian cookery is that two people set out to cook a particular dish, using identical ingredients and applying the same methods, but almost invariably they manage to get different results!

The cookery artistes of India are not known for their enthusiasm and generosity to share their knowledge with others. The best source of information in this regard is usually the old relatives who always have the secrets of some marvellous recipes tucked away in the vaults of their memories. I am lucky to hail from Lal Phatak, my family home in Kanpur, which houses under one roof the whole

Pandya clan, complete with all the old grans and wizened old grand-uncles! Besides, my family is full of excellent cooks anyway. My mother, who was always my main source of inspiration, was a superb cook, and my father a discerning connoisseur of good food. By a sheer stroke of luck, my wife too is a magnificent cook, and so are my mother-in-law, my sisters, my aunts and so forth! But, unlike other Indian chefs, I have no compunction about parting with tradition and sharing my recipes with you!

Measure of hotness in Indian food

People often ask me whether a particular Indian dish is 'hot'. Frankly, it is not an easy question to answer because 'hot', 'medium' and 'mild' are *relative* descriptions of a dish's hotness. In southern India, for instance, a mild curry is hotter than the hot curries of the north, and vice versa.

Unless otherwise stated in the recipes, all dishes in this book are of medium hotness – my medium. The best advice I can offer is that you should find your own level of acceptance, like in everything else in Indian cookery, and that then becomes your 'medium'. Increase the chilli content (or use whole spices, instead of powders) and you have a hot dish; decrease it, and you have a mild dish. Adjustments are, however, frequently called for where other people are involved.

There are, of course, some dishes that are traditionally hot or mild, eg. vindaloos, or pullaos and biriyanis respectively, but that is not to say that their chilli content cannot be adapted according to requirement! It is nonsense to say that Indian food is always hot, or that it has got to be hot to be good. The flavour and taste of a dish are of paramount importance for everyone; hotness or mildness is a matter of personal choice.

Freezing

With regard to freezing Indian food, kebabs and samosas can be frozen for a few months if made in large quantities, and thawed and cooked when required. Cooked meat dishes can be stored in a refrigerator, to be reheated and served later. Having said that, Indian food should be made fresh every time, or one or two days in advance. I would not like to encourage wholesale freezing of foods, as spices generally do not freeze well.

Ingredients

First class ingredients in all dishes must always be used in order to get the best results. Substitutes should only be used when advised. You may find the list of ingredients in some of the recipes a bit daunting but on closer scrutiny you will notice that many of them are spices.

All ingredients, including the vegetables, are available in most Asian grocery shops. If you have difficulty in obtaining any particular ingredient ask the managers of Indian restaurants in your neighbourhood. Between them everything should be available except the seasonal vegetables out of season. I have noticed a pleasing recent trend, that Indian green vegetables and fresh herbs, such as coriander, are sold in many ordinary supermarkets now.

After cooking a splendid meal you should enjoy it in convivial company. A good Indian meal has a salubrious effect on your health and happiness – you feel a new person. A blend of good food, conversation and soft music usually create a perfect setting for a leisurely Indian meal. I have already taken up too much of your time in this chit-chat and have no wish to stand any longer between you and your captivating kitchen delights. Bon appetit!

Michael Pandya

Cardiff
1983

7

PRESENTATION OF FOOD

It is customary in India to serve all the dishes of the meal together at the outset; the meal is served on a metal salver in several small metal bowls. Also, by tradition, Indian food is normally eaten sitting down. And the drink at the end of a meal is water – not wine; you could perhaps make an exception in the case of champagne! Over the years the scenario has changed considerably; these days Indian get-togethers are conducted in buffet style. Besides, western style crockery and cutlery are now in general use in Indian homes and there is now a tendency to pool the food centrally, so that the guests can help themselves.

Indian meals can of course be vegetarian or non-vegetarian; they can also be very substantial meals or light-weight ones. When serving the meal, make sure that your menu is balanced, not only in terms of the nutritious value of the food but also from the point of view of flavour and texture. Make sure that the combination of dishes complement each other. The secret is to offer a wide choice, so that your guests can pick and choose, and for there to be enough to please the 'fire eaters' as well as those who like milder food with plenty of flavour, but no 'kick'.

Try to create an Indian ambience in your dining room. Arrange fresh flowers and burn a few joss-sticks. Play soft Indian music before, during and after the meal. Make a feature of your dining table by spreading an Indian style table-cloth over it and arrange the napkins in glasses in the shape of flowers. Arrange the food neatly on the table so that it is easy for the guests to pick and choose the dishes of their choice, whether vegetarian or non-vegetarian.

Serve your soups with sippets (see page 17) to add style and texture to them; add single or double cream for variety. Garnish the main dishes with slices of square tomatoes and eggs – made specially by filling square moulds with beaten eggs and pulp of tomatoes, and then baking them – and red radishes, to lend colour to your dishes. For serving raitas and chutneys, make containers out of pineapples having first scooped out the flesh, and delight your guests.

If you are serving soft drinks, reserve some of it and freeze it in advance to make ice cubes; add these coloured ice cubes to the drinks when serving. On a scorching summer day, these drinks will make your guests feel cool and thankful. Make tiny buckets out of satsumas – by removing the flesh and cutting the peel into appropriate shapes and serve puddings and desserts in them. Decorate and arrange sweetmeats with edible Indian gold and silver foils in order to give your dining room a look of affluence and gaiety. Serve Indian ice creams by slicing them in an imaginative fashion and serving them in bowls of contrasting colours.

As host you should give a lead to your guests by arranging the food in such a way that everyone starts with soup/samosa/pakoda/chaat, then goes on to the main dishes – rice/breads, vegetarian or non-vegetarian curries and dry dishes together with poppadums, raita/chutney/pickles – and concludes with an ice cream/soft drink/pudding/sweetmeat/fresh fruit. You should then say farewell to your guests with an offer of paan and all its accompaniments (see page 129). To add a festive touch you can decorate the paan with edible silver foils.

I give below a few sample menus.

1
a non-vegetarian pakoda
a meat dish, eg. a vindaloo
Indian bread: paraunthas,
poppadums or fries
pickles, chutney and raita
a sweet, eg. dall sweet in syrup
paan and accompaniments

2
a non-vegetarian soup
a non-vegetarian pullao or biriyani
a raita
poppadums
a sweet, eg. coconut balls
paan and accompaniments

3
a vegetarian soup
puri: plain or stuffed
a vegetarian curry, eg. a kofta curry
two dry vegetables, including a
stuffed one
poppadums or fries
dall dumplings in yoghurt
chutney and pickles
a pudding
paan and accompaniments

4
a vegetarian soup
rice and split green beans
poppadums
pickles and cabbage raita
a sweet, eg. sweet yoghurt in saffron
paan and accompaniments

5
a vegetarian samosa
chapaatis
boiled rice
dall
two dry vegetables, including a
'whole' dish
poppadums, chutney and pickles
a sweet
paan and accompaniments

6
Puffed rice chaat
flour wafers
dosa
poppadums or fries
an ice cream or soft drink
paan and accompaniments

7
a vegetarian samosa
aubergine chaat
dried peas chaat
potato chops
fries
dall dumplings in yoghurt
spiced tea
paan and accompaniments

8
a non-vegetarian soup
a non-vegetarian samosa
spiced chicken drumsticks
stuffed eggs
fries
a hot drink
paan and accompaniments

WEIGHTS AND MEASURES
NAAP AUR TAUL

The experienced cooks of India do not normally talk in terms of exact weights and measures; they usually guess the quantities of ingredients to be used and invariably get first class results. That of course would not be a proper way to introduce you to a new cuisine. Therefore quantities have been given for all recipes in metric, imperial and American. However, because the exact conversions do not always result in convenient working quantities, the conversion figures given in this book are approximate and generally have been rounded off. *Use either the metric or imperial measures as they are not interchangeable.*

It is imperative that you find your level of acceptance for some of the strong ingredients first, and then adapt the quantities to your taste. The most important in this connection are: chillies, garlic, salt, sugar, sugar syrup, ginger, whole and/or powdered spices. To that extent, the weights and measures of these ingredients given in the recipes are for your general guidance only.

WEIGHTS

IMPERIAL	METRIC
1oz	25g
2oz	50g
3oz	75g
4oz (¼lb)	100g
6oz	175g
8oz (½lb)	225g
16oz (1lb)	450g
18oz	500g
20oz (1¼lb)	575g
35oz	1000g (1 kilogramme)

LIQUID MEASURES

IMPERIAL	METRIC
2 tablespoons (1fl oz)	30ml
¼ pint (5fl oz)	150ml
½ pint (10fl oz)	300ml
1 pint (20fl oz)	600ml
1¾ pints (30fl oz)	1000ml (1 litre)

SPOON MEASURES

1 teaspoon	= 1 teaspoon
1½ teaspoons	= 1 dessertspoon
3 teaspoons	= 1 tablespoon

For American and Australian readers

It is important to remember that the Australian tablespoon differs from the British and American tablespoons. The British standard tablespoon holds 17.7 millilitres, the British metric tablespoon holds 15 millilitres, the American 14.2 millilitres, and the Australian 20 millilitres. A teaspoon holds about 5 millilitres in all three countries.

OVEN TEMPERATURES

DESCRIPTION	DEGREES CENTIGRADE	DEGREES FAHRENHEIT	GAS MARK
Very cool	110	225	¼
	120	250	½
Cool	140	275	1
	150	300	2
Moderate	160	325	3
	180	350	4
Moderately hot	190	375	5
	200	400	6
Hot	220	425	7
	230	450	8
Very hot	240	475	9

BRITISH	AMERICAN	AUSTRALIAN
1 teaspoon	1 teaspoon	1 teaspoon
1 dessertspoon	1 dessertspoon	1 dessertspoon
1 tablespoon	1 tablespoon	1 tablespoon
1½ tablespoons	2 tablespoons	1½ tablespoons
2 tablespoons	3 tablespoons	2 tablespoons
3½ tablespoons	4 tablespoons	3 tablespoons
4 tablespoons	5 tablespoons	3½ tablespoons

The imperial pint, 20fl oz, is used in Britain and Australia; in America the pint holds 16fl oz. Both America and Australia use the 250ml/8fl oz measuring cup; Australia uses it in conjunction with metric measures.

COOKING UTENSILS
CHAUKE KE BARTAN

When cooking Indian food, you should try and adopt a totally Indian mood in your kitchen. Among other things, do make an effort to obtain and use some of the more commonly used utensils and tools used in a traditional Indian kitchen. Quite a few of them seem to be easily available in the United Kingdom and other countries of the West.

There is no denying the fact that many western utensils and tools are as appropriate, if not more so in some cases, as the Indian ones themselves. The frying pan and saucepan can easily be substituted for the *tawa* and the *batloi*; a wooden spatula is in fact more welcome than the metal *karchhi*.

As a general guidance here, you should avoid the contact of metals and spices as far as possible. But not all metals are to be avoided; enamelled metal pots and pans and other tools, for instance, are quite suitable and are widely used. So are the tools and utensils made of stainless steel.

Listed below are the tools and utensils that are an integral part of an Indian kitchen:

Batloi — Also known as *pateeli* or *degchi*, a suitable metal cooking pot; saucepans can be used instead.

Chakla-belan — A wooden rolling (bread) board and rolling pin, used for rolling out thin rounds of dough and pastry.

Chamcha — A metal scoop, resembling a ladle; used for serving soups and curried dishes.

Chhalni — A metal or wooden sieve; used for straining flours and liquids.

Chimta — A pair of long and flat tongs, with blunt edges; normally used for turning over chapaatis and for picking up small food items being roasted.

Jhanna — A metal spoon with a long handle, and a perforated disc at the end; used for draining foods before they are taken out of a *kadhai*, or deep fryer, after frying, and also when making a batter of 'dropping' consistency.

Kaddu-kas — A grater, used for many varieties of thin and thick gratings.

Kadhai — A deep, wide-mouthed, metal pan with handles on both sides; looks something like a Chinese wok. Used for deep frying, and making halwas as well as moist and dry vegetable preparations. A deep fryer or frying pan may be used instead.

Karchhi — A metal spoon with a long handle and a flat disc at the end of it. Used as a stirrer. A wooden spatula may be used instead.

Khalla-musaria — Also known as imaamdusta-aur-daanti; roughly equates with the pestle and mortar. Made of cast iron,

11

| | clay or enamel, comes in various shapes and sizes and is used for pounding hard ingredients. For larger quantities, an electric grinder may be used. | | *sil* – a large stone slab with a rough surface – and then pressed by the *batta* – the small round stone with a rough surface. See also *Khalla-musaria.* |

Mathaani
A wooden hand-whisk; used for whisking milk, buttermilk and yoghurt for various drinks and curried dishes.

Sil-batta
A pair of treated stones used for grinding herbs and spices. The ingredients are placed over the

Taraazu
A pair of scales for weighing ingredients.

Tawa
A griddle, invariably made of cast-iron. Generally used for making chapaatis and paraunthas, and for roasting spices. A heavy frying pan may be used instead.

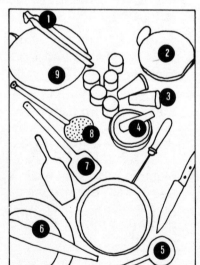

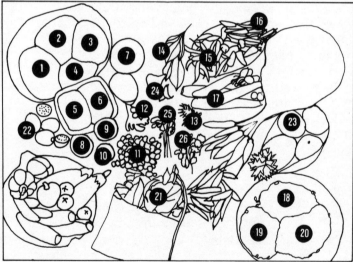

Right Indian cooking utensils
1: Chimta (tongs) 2: Kadhai (metal pan with handles used for frying) 3: Ice cream moulds 4: Imamdusta aur daanti (pestle and mortar) 5: Chamcha (a ladle) 6: Chakla-belan (rolling board and rolling pin) 7: Karchhi (spatula) 8: Jhanna (draining spoon) 9: Tawa (griddle)

Overleaf Selection of vegetables and pulses
1: Moong dall 2: Split moong 3: Puffed rice 4: Split red lentils (masoor dall) 5: Basmati rice 6: Patna rice 7: Toor dall (pigeon peas) 8: Moong 9: Black beans (urad) 10: Urad dall 11: Lotus puffs (makhaana) 12: Root ginger 13: Curry leaves 14: Bay leaves 15: Chillis 16: Okra 17: Indian radishes 18: Batter drops (boondi) 19: Grams (bhoora chana) 20: Flattened rice (chewda) 21: Spinach 22: Tamarina 23: Mangoes 24: Garlic 25: Fenugreek 26: Coriander

BASIC RECIPES
JAADU KI POTLI

The master chefs of India over the centuries have evolved techniques and 'special' ingredients, largely unknown in the West, which seem 'magical' and which are essentially responsible for the exotic nature of Indian food. These special preparations, when mixed with other more well-known cookery ingredients, unleash a typically Indian culinary chemistry which produces tantalising tastes and fabulous flavours in food. Some of these ingredients, which make Indian cuisine unique and give it such an enviable reputation, are described in this section.

Clarified butter

Ghee
●

Although expensive, **ghee** *is the traditional and the best medium for frying Indian food. You can heat it to a high temperature and thereby guarantee crisp results.*
Ghee *is easy to make at home and lasts for months!*
It is also available ready-prepared at Indian grocers.

Preparation time 10 minutes	**Cooking time 25 minutes**	**Makes 450g/1lb/2 cups**

METRIC/IMPERIAL	AMERICAN
575g/1¼lb butter	2½ cups butter

Melt the butter in a heavy-based saucepan over a moderate heat. Bring to the boil, stirring constantly. Lower the heat and simmer for about 20 minutes until the moisture has evaporated and the protein and impurities have settled at the bottom.

Remove the pan from the heat and, using a wooden spatula, remove the scum from the top. Carefully strain the contents into a covered container – discarding the salty residue at the bottom of the pan – and leave to cool; it will set as it cools.

Left Breads and fries (from the top clockwise) Chapaati (see page 30) Flour wafers – golgappa (see page 61) Poppadums (see page 25) Rice flour fries (see page 27) Parauntha (see page 31)

Tandoori powder

Tandoori masala

*This powder is responsible to a considerable extent for the exotic flavour and superb
taste of the Indian tandoori dishes (made in a clay oven); particularly used for chicken
dishes and also for spicing tikkas and steaks.*

Preparation time 5 minutes   **Makes about 50g/2oz/½ cup**

METRIC/IMPERIAL	AMERICAN
1 teaspoon garlic powder	1 teaspoon garlic powder
1 teaspoon ground ginger	1 teaspoon ground ginger
1 teaspoon cloves powder	1 teaspoon cloves powder
1 teaspoon mace powder	1 teaspoon mace powder
½ teaspoon grated nutmeg	½ teaspoon grated nutmeg
2 tablespoons ground coriander	3 tablespoons ground coriander
1½ teaspoons cumin powder	1½ teaspoons cumin powder
1 teaspoon fenugreek powder	1 teaspoon fenugreek powder
1 teaspoon ground cinnamon	1 teaspoon ground cinnamon
1 teaspoon freshly ground black pepper	1 teaspoon freshly ground black pepper
1 teaspoon ground brown cardamom seeds	1 teaspoon ground brown cardamom seeds
2 teaspoons red food colouring	2 teaspoons red food coloring

Mix all the above ingredients, without roasting them first, and push through a fine sieve. Store in an airtight container. Close the lid tightly after each use. Tandoori powder can also be purchased ready-made.

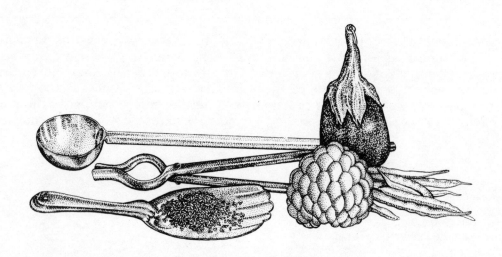

Vindaloo powder

Vindaloo masala

●

A hot powder used to make vindaloo dishes.
This can be bought ready-made but the home-prepared variety is superior.

Preparation time 10 minutes   **Cooking time about 10 minutes**

METRIC/IMPERIAL	AMERICAN
2 tablespoons pounded dried red chillies or red chilli powder	3 tablespoons pounded dried red chillies or red chilli powder
1 tablespoon black peppercorns	1 tablespoon black peppercorns
1 tablespoon cloves	1 tablespoon cloves
2 tablespoons mustard seeds	3 tablespoons mustard seeds
50g/2oz coriander seeds	6 tablespoons coriander seeds
1 tablespoon fenugreek seeds	1 tablespoon fenugreek seeds
2 tablespoons ground cinnamon	3 tablespoons ground cinnamon
2 tablespoons turmeric powder	3 tablespoons turmeric powder
1 tablespoon brown cardamom powder	1 tablespoon brown cardamom powder
10 bay leaves	10 bay leaves

Heat a griddle or heavy frying pan over a moderate heat and roast all the ingredients until they give off an aromatic smell. Remove from the heat and grind by hand or in an electric grinder into a powder.

Press the powder through a fine muslin cloth, or fine sieve.

Store in an airtight container to keep fresh. Cover tightly after each use. (For example of use, see page 90.)

Saambhar powder

Saambhar masala

•

This powder saves a lot of eleventh hour work towards preparing saambhar
*(see page 107), the vegetable sauce, normally served with dosa dishes
(see page 66) and also with some other south Indian dishes.*

Preparation time 10 minutes   **Cooking time 10 minutes**

METRIC/IMPERIAL	AMERICAN
4 tablespoons pigeon peas *(toor dall)*	5 tablespoons *toor dall* (pigeon peas)
2 tablespoons mustard seeds	3 tablespoons mustard seeds
100g/4oz coriander seeds	¼lb coriander seeds
1 tablespoon fenugreek seeds	1 tablespoon fenugreek seeds
1 tablespoon carom seeds	1 tablespoon carom seeds
2 teaspoons black peppercorns	2 teaspoons black peppercorns
1 tablespoon dry curry leaves, crushed	1 tablespoon dry curry leaves, crushed
1 tablespoon red chilli powder	1 tablespoon red chilli powder
1 tablespoon turmeric powder	1 tablespoon turmeric powder
1 teaspoon asafoetida powder	1 teaspoon asafoetida powder

Heat a griddle or heavy frying pan over a moderate heat and roast all the ingredients for about 10 minutes until they give off a strong aromatic smell. Remove from the heat and coarsely grind by hand or in an electric grinder.

Store in an airtight container. Cover tightly after each use.

Mixed spice powder
Garam masala

Garam masala is a vital ingredient for many Indian savoury dishes.
Although available ready-made I would recommend that you make
your own. Curiously, most Indian chefs have their own recipes for it.

Preparation time 10 minutes   Cooking time 10 minutes

METRIC/IMPERIAL	AMERICAN
25g/1oz coriander seeds	3 tablespoons coriander seeds
25g/1oz cloves	3 tablespoons cloves
25g/1oz black peppercorns	¼ cup black peppercorns
25g/1oz cinnamon sticks	1oz cinnamon sticks
25g/1oz brown cardamoms	2 tablespoons brown cardamoms
4 bay leaves	4 bay leaves

Heat a griddle or heavy frying pan over a moderate heat and roast all the ingredients for about 10 minutes until they give off a strong aromatic smell. Remove from the heat and grind by hand or in an electric grinder. Push through a muslin cloth or fine sieve. Store in an airtight container. As long as you close the lid tightly after each use, the garam masala should remain fresh and usable for 2–3 months.

Sippets
Tale gutke

Sippets, also known as croûtons, add a decorative touch when served with soups.
They can be made and stored in advance.

Preparation time 8 minutes   Cooking time about 2 minutes per batch

METRIC/IMPERIAL	AMERICAN
2 thick slices of bread	2 thick slices of bread
ghee for deep frying	ghee for deep frying

Remove the crusts from the bread and cut into small cubes.

Heat the ghee in a *kadhai* or deep fryer to almost smoking point. Fry the bread cubes for about 2 minutes until golden all over. When cooked, remove and drain on absorbent kitchen paper.

Cool and store the sippets in an airtight container. When required, do not leave them in the open for long.

Home-made cream cheese

Chhena aur paneer

Chhena *is the popular base for making many mouth-watering Bengali sweetmeats; in the Punjab,* paneer *is used for making curries and other savouries.*

Preparation time 15 minutes   Cooking time 5 minutes   Makes about 100g/4oz

METRIC/IMPERIAL	AMERICAN
600ml/1 pint creamy milk	2½ cups creamy milk
juice of ½ lemon	juice of ½ lemon

Place the milk in a saucepan and bring to the boil. Remove from the heat and stir the milk until cool. Add the lemon juice and keep stirring until the milk coagulates.

Pour the curdled milk through a muslin cloth, draw the corners together to make a bag and squeeze out the liquid. The remainder is *chhena*. It should weigh about 100g/4oz. Keep in a bowl and use for making sweetmeats.

To make *paneer*, you should mould the cheese into a block and press under a heavy object until it sets. Cut into squares or diamond shapes, as desired, and use for savoury recipes.

Indian yoghurt

Dahi

Indian yoghurt plays a versatile role in the preparation of many cool, sweet and savoury dishes; and it is not difficult to make at home.

**Preparation time 10 minutes plus setting time   Cooking time 5 minutes
Makes about 1 litre/1¾ pints/4¼ cups**

METRIC/IMPERIAL	AMERICAN
1 litre/1¾ pints milk	4¼ cups milk
4 tablespoons plain yoghurt	⅓ cup plain yoghurt

Place the milk in a saucepan and bring to the boil. Cool for a few minutes.

Beat the yoghurt thoroughly and stir into the milk while still warm. Transfer the mixture from one container to another. Repeat this process several times, in quick succession. Pour the contents into a deep bowl, cover and leave in a warm place overnight. Yoghurt is then ready to use.

Dried milk

Khoya or Mawa

●

The importance of khoya *can hardly be exaggerated as many Indian sweetmeats and desserts are* khoya-*based.*
In the past I have written detailed recipes for this vital ingredient which entailed lengthy boiling of milk. Now witness the quickest and the easiest of them all!

Preparation time 5 minutes

METRIC/IMPERIAL	AMERICAN
4 tablespoons full cream milk powder	5 tablespoons full cream milk powder
2 tablespoons water	3 tablespoons water

Place the milk powder and water in a deep bowl, mix throughly and you have khoya!

You can also buy in Asian grocers in block form but it is better to make your own.

Sugar syrup

Chaashni

●

Sugar syrup is used in the preparation of many Indian sweetmeats. Sugar candy (misree) *is available in packets at Indian grocers.*

Preparation time 5 minutes   **Cooking time about 15 minutes**

METRIC/IMPERIAL	AMERICAN
600ml/1 pint water	2½ cups water
450g/1lb sugar	2 cups sugar

Pour and mix the water and sugar in a deep saucepan over moderate heat and bring to the boil. Lower the heat and continue cooking. Remove and discard the scum from the top from time to time.

When pressed between your thumb and forefinger, a drop of syrup lifts up in one string, it is known as one-string syrup. This strength of the syrup is usually adequate for many sweets and takes about 15 minutes to make.

You may go on cooking further in order to get a 2, 3 or 4-string syrup. Eventually the syrup will crack into chips, forming sugar candy *(misree).* This is also available ready-made.

Special gravy

Shorwa

●

The gravy made according to this recipe can be used to curry dry dishes,
eg. kofta curries.

Preparation time 10 minutes   Cooking time 25 minutes   Makes 300ml/½ pint/1¼ cups

METRIC/IMPERIAL	AMERICAN
100g/4oz ghee	½ cup ghee
1 large onion, finely chopped	1 large onion, finely chopped
1 teaspoon turmeric powder	1 teaspoon turmeric powder
1 teaspoon red chilli powder	1 teaspoon red chilli powder
1 teaspoon ground coriander	1 teaspoon ground coriander
2 cloves garlic, crushed	2 cloves garlic, crushed
½ teaspoon grated fresh ginger root	½ teaspoon grated fresh ginger root
2 tablespoons tomato purée	3 tablespoons tomato paste
2 tablespoons plain yoghurt	3 tablespoons plain yoghurt
300ml/½ pint warm water	1¼ cups warm water
½ teaspoon salt	½ teaspoon salt

Heat the ghee in a saucepan and fry the onion until golden. Stir in turmeric, chilli, coriander, garlic and ginger and blend thoroughly. Then gradually add the tomato purée and yoghurt. Stir continuously for about 5 minutes until the ghee separates from the spices. Pour in the water and salt, bring to the boil and simmer for about 10 minutes. Use as required.

SOUPS
SOOP

Although the Indians have always drunk *shorwas* in the North and *rassams* in southern India – juices made from a wide variety of dalls, vegetables and meats – the soup dish in its present form made its formal debut in India with the advent of the Raj. The British army officers insisted on a traditional appetiser before their main meal. This custom ultimately led to the creation of soups as we know them today.

However, in India soups are often served as light meals or snacks and not always as starters before a main meal.

Carrot soup
Gaajar ka soop

Preparation time 10 minutes **Cooking time 30 minutes** **Serves 4**

METRIC/IMPERIAL	AMERICAN
1 tablespoon ghee	1 tablespoon ghee
4 large carrots, diced	4 large carrots, diced
1 small onion, chopped	1 small onion, chopped
1 small potato, quartered	1 small potato, quartered
300ml/½ pint vegetable stock	1¼ cups vegetable stock or broth
600ml/1 pint water	2½ cups water
4 tablespoons milk	⅓ cup milk
2 teaspoons salt or to taste	2 teaspoons salt or to taste
1 teaspoon freshly ground black pepper	1 teaspoon freshly ground black pepper
double cream, to serve	heavy cream, to serve

Heat the ghee in a saucepan and lightly fry all the vegetables. Pour in the stock and water, cover and cook over a moderate heat for about 20 minutes until the vegetables are tender. Remove from the heat, mash the vegetables well into the liquid and strain into another pan. Add the milk and seasoning and cook for another 5 minutes. Serve steaming hot, topped with cream or yoghurt and croûtons *(sippets)*, if desired. (For photograph see page 44.)

Green pea soup

Hari matar ka soop

Preparation time 5 minutes   **Cooking time 25 minutes**   **Serves 4**

METRIC/IMPERIAL	AMERICAN
225g/8oz green peas	1⅓ cups green peas
300ml/½ pint water	1¼ cups water
600ml/1 pint vegetable stock	2½ cups vegetable stock or broth
salt to taste	salt to taste
1 teaspoon freshly ground black pepper	1 teaspoon freshly ground black pepper
single cream, to serve	light cream, to serve

Place the peas and water in a saucepan, bring to the boil and simmer for about 15 minutes until tender. Remove from the heat, mash the peas well into the liquid and sieve into another saucepan.

Place the pan over a moderate heat and add the stock and seasoning. Bring to the boil and then remove from the heat. Serve boiling hot with 1 tablespoon cream added to each serving.

Bacon soup

Bekan ka soop

Preparation time 10 minutes   **Cooking time 35 minutes**   **Serves 4**

METRIC/IMPERIAL	AMERICAN
450g/1lb streaky bacon, chopped	1lb bacon slices, chopped
900ml/1½ pints water	3¾ cups water
1 small onion, chopped	1 small onion, chopped
2 large tomatoes, halved	2 large tomatoes, halved
2 cloves garlic, sliced	2 cloves garlic, sliced
salt to taste	salt to taste
2 tablespoons cornflour	3 tablespoons cornstarch
½ teaspoon freshly ground black pepper	½ teaspoon freshly ground black pepper
whipped double cream, to serve	whipped heavy cream, to serve

Place all the ingredients, except the cream, in a large saucepan and bring to the boil. Remove the scum from the top, from time to time, until the soup is clear.

Lower the heat, half cover the pan and simmer for about 20 minutes. Strain through muslin, if desired, and serve steaming hot, topped with the cream.

Prawn soup

Jheenga paani

Preparation time 10 minutes   Cooking time 30 minutes   Serves 4

METRIC/IMPERIAL	AMERICAN
600ml/1 pint prawns, washed and peeled	2½ cups shrimps, washed and shelled
¼ teaspoon grated fresh ginger root	¼ teaspoon grated fresh ginger root
2 tomatoes, chopped	2 tomatoes, chopped
900ml/1½ pints water	3¾ cups water
4 tablespoons chopped onion	5 tablespoons chopped onion
2 teaspoons salt or to taste	2 teaspoons salt or to taste
1 teaspoon freshly ground black pepper	1 teaspoon freshly ground black pepper
1 tablespoon ghee	1 tablespoon ghee
1 teaspoon cornflour	1 teaspoon cornstarch
sippets (see page 17) to serve	sippets (see page 17) to serve

Place the prawns, ginger, tomatoes and water with half of the onion in a deep saucepan. Add the seasoning, bring to the boil and simmer for about 15 minutes. Remove from the heat, strain the liquid through a sieve and reserve the prawns.

Heat the ghee in a separate saucepan and fry the remaining onion and the cornflour (over a moderate heat) for 2–3 minutes. Pour in the broth, bring to the boil and simmer for about 10 minutes. Add reserved prawns and serve piping hot with sippets added to each serving.
(For photograph see page 100.)

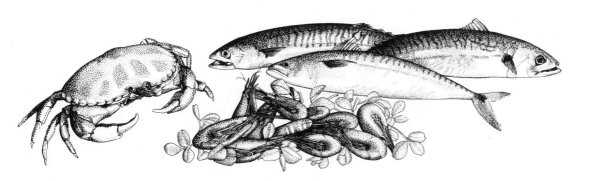

POPPADUMS, FRIES AND BREADS
PAAPAD, KACHRIYAAN AUR ROTIYAAN

In this section of the book, we are going to look at all the weird and wonderful types of bread in Indian cuisine. Some of these can be made in advance and cooked very quickly just before the meal is going to be served, while others can be served as light meals, taken on picnics or arranged to make a feature on your dining table.

Poppadums
Paapad

The poppadum is a very light-weight dish. There are many varieties from paper-thin to fairly thick; from bland to blazing hot! They can be served by themselves or with a meal. The making of poppadums is a speciality of Indian cuisine. Some families spend generations in perfecting this art. You can buy them in packets from your supermarket or Asian grocer, but there are varieties of poppadums you can easily make at home, without any specialist knowledge or experience. I offer here a few recipes which I hope you will find useful. Make and store them in advance and cook them as and when required.

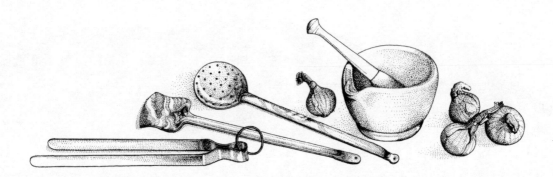

Cooking poppadums
Paapad pakaane ka tarika

•

Poppadums can be cooked in many ways, depending on personal choice; you could cook them under a grill, bake in the oven or deep fry. The most popular method is deep frying.

Preparation time 5 minutes   **Cooking time about 10 seconds each**   **Serves 4**

METRIC/IMPERIAL	AMERICAN
4 poppadums, halved if liked oil for deep frying	4 poppadums, halved if liked oil for deep frying

Heat the oil nearly to smoking point in a pan (test by dropping a little piece in the oil, and if it sizzles immediately, the oil is ready) and slide a poppadum into it. Press with a ladle or spatula for a few seconds, turn over and do the same again before taking out of the pan. This enables the poppadum to spread to its fullest extent; it does not curl up, either.

When the poppadum is cooked, remove from the pan and stand on absorbent kitchen paper to drain off excess fat. Serve hot and crisp. (For photograph see page 77.)

Potato poppadums
Aalu ke paapad

Preparation time 20 minutes plus drying time   **Cooking time 10 minutes**   **Makes 16**

METRIC/IMPERIAL	AMERICAN
1kg/2lb potatoes, boiled and peeled 2 teaspoons salt pinch of bicarbonate of soda 2 teaspoons red chilli powder ghee or oil, to grease	2lb potatoes, boiled and peeled 2 teaspoons salt dash of baking powder 2 teaspoons red chilli powder ghee or oil, to grease

Mix the potatoes, salt, soda and chilli powder together to form a dough. Divide the mixture into 16 or more portions. Grease a flat surface, eg. bread board, and roll out each one into a very thin round.

When all the rounds are made, spread them out on a greased plastic sheet to dry on both sides in the sun or warmest place in the house. When dry store in a covered container, until required. Cook just before use.

Black bean poppadums

Urad ki dall ke paapad

•

Red chilli powder could be used instead of black peppercorns, or for a milder poppadum,
do not use either.

Preparation time 15 minutes plus drying time   **Cooking time 10 minutes**   **Makes 16**

METRIC/IMPERIAL	AMERICAN
450g/1lb black bean *(urad dall)* powder	4 cups black bean *(urad dall)* powder
1 teaspoon salt	1 teaspoon salt
½ teaspoon black peppercorns	½ teaspoon black peppercorns
pinch of asafoetida powder	dash of asafoetida powder
½ teaspoon white cumin seeds	½ teaspoon white cumin seeds
pinch of bicarbonate of soda	dash of baking soda

Place all the ingredients in a mortar and pound thoroughly with the pestle, or use an electric grinder. Add sufficient water to make into a stiff dough. Divide the mixture into 16 portions. Roll out each one into a very thin round. Spread them out on a greased plastic sheet to dry on both sides in the sun or warmest place in the house.

When dry, collect them and store in a clean bag or covered container. Deep fry just before use.

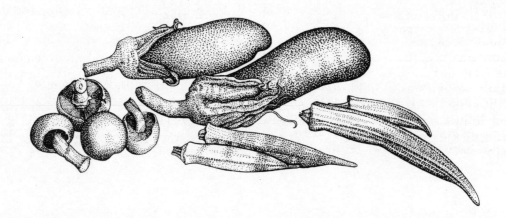

Fries and similar savouries

Kachriyaan aur chut-put

Fries are a very light variety of Indian savoury, made and stored in advance. Useful for that unexpected guest as they can be cooked in seconds! Fries are always deep fried and usually served with a sprinkling of preferred condiments on each serving. Many varieties of fries are commercially available in packets from most Asian grocery shops.

The savouries are normally cooked in advance and can be served cold. They serve as light meals by themselves, have a reputation for bridging the gaps of peckishness between meals and can be taken on picnics. They also go down well with Indian drinks (and aperitifs).

Rice flour fries

Chaawal ki kachri

Preparation time 5 minutes plus drying time   **Cooking time 20 minutes**

METRIC/IMPERIAL	AMERICAN
225g/8oz rice flour	2 cups rice flour
1.15 litres/2 pints water	5 cups water
½ teaspoon salt	½ teaspoon salt
pinch of bicarbonate of soda	dash of baking soda
1 tablespoon arrowroot	1 tablespoon arrowroot
ghee, to grease	ghee, to grease

Put the rice flour, salt, bicarbonate of soda and arrowroot into a saucepan and very gradually beat in the water to make a smooth mixture. Place over a low to moderate heat and cook for about 5 minutes, stirring continuously until the mixture has thickened. Great care must be taken to avoid lumps forming – you must keep stirring all the time.

Grease a platter with the ghee and drop small amounts of the rice paste on to it. Make desired shapes, eg. round blobs, long strands like vermicelli, little chips or flat rounds. Spread them out to dry completely in the warmest place in the house (for several hours). Store in an airtight container. Deep fry in ghee or oil when required. (For photograph see page 13.)

Savoury pancake

Parati sohaal

●

This light snack is a suitable candidate for picnics and parties; it also goes down well with tea or Indian soft drinks.

Preparation time 15 minutes   **Cooking time 15 minutes**   **Serves 6**

METRIC/IMPERIAL	AMERICAN
175g/6oz plain flour	1½ cups all-purpose flour
salt to taste	salt to taste
½ teaspoon carom seeds	½ teaspoon carom seeds
50g/2oz ghee	¼ cup ghee
oil for frying	oil for frying

Mix the flour, salt and carom seeds together in a deep bowl. Rub in the ghee and add sufficient water to make a pliable dough. Divide the dough into 6 portions. Roll each one into a ball, flatten and then roll out into a thin round. Bruise the round all over with the flat blade of a sharp knife and fold in half; do not press the edges. Fold the round over once more and bruise again. Heat the oil in a *kadhai* or deep fryer. Fry the pancakes, a few at a time, taking care not to break them, until they are golden. Remove and drain on absorbent kitchen paper. Serve hot or cold.

Right Selection of spices
1: Bay leaves 2: Asafoetida 3: Cloves 4: Cinnamon sticks 5: Ground ginger 6: Black peppercorns 7: Red chillis 8: Chilli powder 9: Curry leaves 10: Garam masala 11: Green cardamom 12: Cumin seeds 13: Brown cardamom 14: Turmeric 15: Ground cumin 16: Mustard seeds 17: Saffron

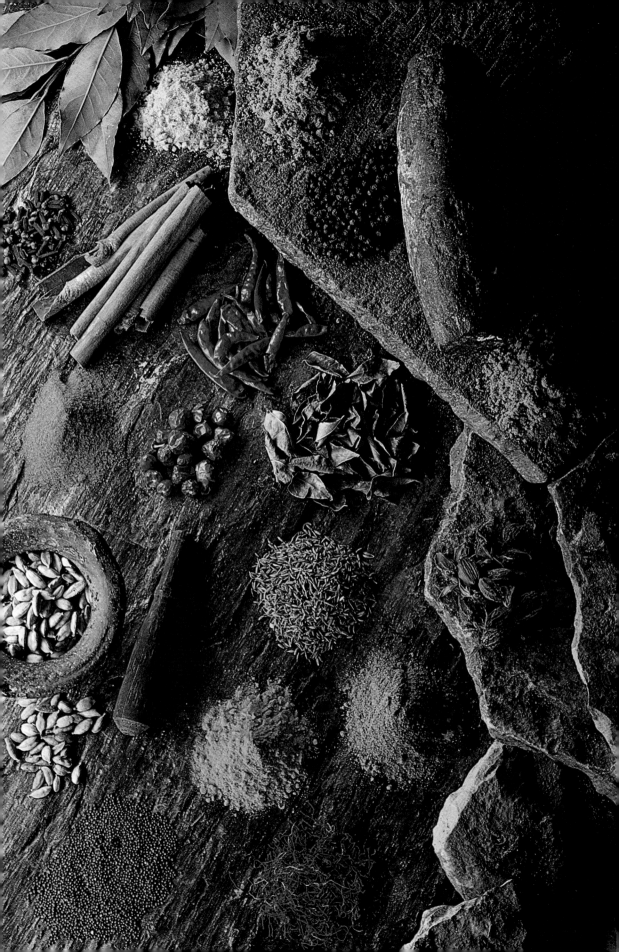

Gram flour crisp rounds
Besan ki papdi

Preparation time 15 minutes plus drying time   **Cooking time 15 minutes**   **Serves 6**

METRIC/IMPERIAL	AMERICAN
225g/8oz gram flour (*besan*)	2 cups gram flour (*besan*)
50g/2oz plain flour	½ cup all-purpose flour
1 teaspoon salt	1 teaspoon salt
1 teaspoon carom seeds	1 teaspoon carom seeds
1 teaspoon red chilli powder	1 teaspoon red chilli powder
50g/2oz ghee	¼ cup ghee
oil for deep frying	oil for deep frying

Rub and mix all the ingredients together and add sufficient water to make a medium consistency dough. Divide the mixture into 12 portions. Roll out each one into a very thin round. Place them to dry in the sun or warmest place in the house.

Heat the oil in a *kadhai* or deep fryer and fry the rounds, about 4 at a time, until they are golden brown and crisp all over. Remove and drain on kitchen paper.

Chewda dallmoth
Chewda dallmoth

Preparation time 5 minutes   **Cooking time 5 minutes**   **Serves 6**

METRIC/IMPERIAL	AMERICAN
225g/8oz ghee	1 cup ghee
225g/8oz flattened rice (*chewda*)	½lb flattened rice (*chewda*)
1 teaspoon salt	1 teaspoon salt
½ teaspoon red chilli powder	½ teaspoon red chilli powder
1 teaspoon mustard seeds, fried	1 teaspoon mustard seeds, fried

Heat the ghee in a *kadhai* or deep fryer to near smoking point and fry the chewda, a little at a time. Chewda puffs up and fries quickly in a few seconds.

After frying each portion, place the chewda on a plate, lined with greaseproof paper. When all the chewda is fried, stir in the salt, chilli powder and mustard seeds and mix thoroughly. When cool, store in an airtight container until required.

Left Savouries and snacks (from the top) Onion Bhaaji (see page 40) Chewda dallmoth (see above) Quicky kebabs (see page 50) Fish croquettes (see page 51)

Indian breads

Hindustaani rotiyaan

The breads of India are a fabulous phenomenon of the country's cuisine. They are generally made from wheat flour or other corns and find favour, in the main, with the inhabitants of the Punjab, Kashmir, Delhi and parts of Uttar Pradesh. While it is true that all the breads in this category cannot be eaten by themselves, it is equally true that without them, meals for many people will not be complete.

The most popular is the chapaati. It is a flat round, made out of a pliable dough, and cooked on a griddle or heavy frying pan, without the use of any cooking fat. Paraunthas are another variety of the Indian bread made out of a medium dough. These are shallow fried in ghee or mustard oil on a griddle. Puris are the third main category of Indian bread. This variety consists of small, flat rounds made out of a stiff dough, which are deep fried.

With a little culinary experimentation, a whole new range of stuffed breads has also been produced. The possibilities are endless; a few samples are suggested in this section.

Chapaati

Chapaati or Tawe ki roti

●

The chapaati is the mainstay of the informal Indian vegetarian meal.

Preparation time 20 minutes   Cooking time 15 minutes   Serves 4

METRIC/IMPERIAL	AMERICAN
450g/1lb wholemeal flour	4 cups wholewheat flour
2 tablespoons plain flour, to dredge	3 tablespoons all-purpose flour, to dredge
100g/4oz ghee, to serve	½ cup ghee, to serve

Place the flour in a bowl and add sufficient water to knead into a pliable dough. Leave to rest for 10 minutes. Splash some more water on to the dough and knead once again. Divide the dough into 12 portions. Roll into balls. Dip each one into the plain flour, flatten and then roll out into 15cm/6-inch rounds.

Heat a griddle or heavy frying pan until very hot. Fry one round, turning over after 10 seconds. Cook for about 20 seconds until brown spots appear all over. Press lightly with absorbent kitchen paper and the chapaati will puff up. Make the other chapaatis in the same way. (You can roast chapaatis over a fire after being cooked on the griddle.) Serve the chapaati hot, with a generous coating of ghee on one side, with a curry or dall. (For photograph see page 13.)

Plain parauntha

Saada parauntha

Paraunthas are sustaining and wholesome.
They can be eaten with a moist vegetable or meat dish.
Punjabis eat them at breakfast with salted yoghurt.

Preparation time 20 minutes   **Cooking time 15 minutes**   **Serves 4**

METRIC/IMPERIAL	AMERICAN
225g/8oz wholemeal flour	2 cups wholewheat flour
pinch of salt	dash of salt
pinch of red chilli powder	dash of red chilli powder
½ teaspoon white cumin seeds	½ teaspoon white cumin seeds
ghee as necessary	ghee as necessary

Place the flour in a bowl and mix in the salt, red chilli powder and cumin. Make a depression in the middle of the flour and pour in sufficient water to knead into a medium consistency dough. Leave to rest for 10 minutes and then knead again. Divide the dough into 8 portions. Roll each one into a ball, flatten, apply some ghee and fold over. Then apply some more ghee and fold again. You will now have a triangular shape. Using a rolling pin, roll out each triangle making 8 thin triangular shapes.

Heat a griddle or heavy frying pan over a moderate heat and grease with ½ teaspoon ghee. Place a parauntha on top.

Apply 1 teaspoon ghee on top of the parauntha and cook for about 30 seconds. Turn it over, apply another teaspoon of ghee and cook for 30 seconds. Turn the parauntha over a couple of times until dark brown spots appear on both sides. Remove and drain on absorbent kitchen paper. Make the other paraunthas in the same way. Serve hot. (For photographs see pages 13 and 100.)

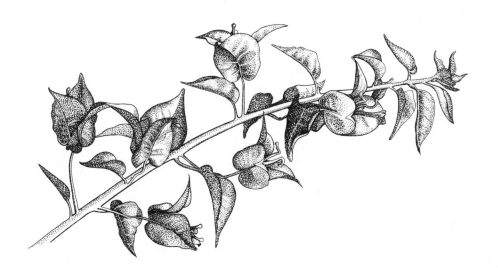

Parauntha with spinach

Saag bhare paraunthe

•

*These substantial and scrumptious breads can be stuffed with either spinach or
fenugreek leaves – or any other leafy vegetable of your choice.*

Preparation time 15–20 minutes	Cooking time 25 minutes	Serves 4

METRIC/IMPERIAL	AMERICAN
225g/8oz spinach, cleaned and finely chopped	½lb spinach, cleaned and finely chopped
1 green chilli, finely chopped	1 green chilli, finely chopped
1 teaspoon chopped coriander leaves	1 teaspoon chopped coriander leaves
½ teaspoon garam masala	½ teaspoon garam masala
1 teaspoon mango powder	1 teaspoon mango powder
½ teaspoon red chilli powder	½ teaspoon red chilli powder
salt to taste	salt to taste
225g/8oz plain flour	2 cups all-purpose flour
ghee as necessary	ghee as necessary

Place the spinach, chilli, coriander, garam masala, mango and chilli powders in a saucepan, add ½ teaspoon salt and a few splashings of water. Cover and steam for 5 minutes. Allow to cool and divide into 8 portions.

Meanwhile, place the flour in a bowl and rub 1 tablespoon ghee and a large pinch of salt. Add sufficient water to knead into a medium consistency dough. Divide into 8 portions. Roll each one into a small ball, then flatten. Add one portion of the filling to each dough round and fold over to enclose it. Brush them with a little ghee and roll out on a floured surface, making triangular shapes.

Heat a griddle or heavy-bottomed frying pan, grease with 1 teaspoon ghee. Place a parauntha on top. Apply 1 teaspoon ghee on top of the parauntha and cook for about 30 seconds. Turn over, apply another teaspoon of ghee and cook for 30 seconds. Turn over a couple of times until brown spots appear on both sides. Remove and drain on absorbent kitchen paper. Make the other paraunthas in the same way. Serve hot with a curry and/or a yoghurt dish.

Parauntha with cauliflower

Gobhi ke parauntha

●

This bread completes a sumptuous meal; serve with a raita or pickle.

Preparation time 15–20 minutes   **Cooking time 20 minutes**   **Serves 4**

METRIC/IMPERIAL	AMERICAN
225g/8oz plain flour	2 cups all-purpose flour
ghee as necessary	ghee as necessary
salt to taste	salt to taste
225g/8oz cauliflower, grated	½lb cauliflower, grated
1 teaspoon mango powder	1 teaspoon mango powder
½ teaspoon white cumin seeds	½ teaspoon white cumin seeds
½ teaspoon red chilli powder	½ teaspoon red chilli powder
1 green chilli, chopped	1 green chilli, chopped
1 teaspoon chopped coriander leaves	1 teaspoon chopped coriander leaves
¼ teaspoon grated fresh ginger root	¼ teaspoon grated fresh ginger root

Place the flour in a bowl and rub in 1 tablespoon ghee. Add ½ teaspoon salt and sufficient water to knead into a medium consistency dough.

Mix the cauliflower, mango powder, cumin, chilli powder, chilli, coriander and ginger together with salt to taste. Heat 1 tablespoon ghee in a pan and fry the mixture for 2 minutes. Cool and divide into 8 portions. (This filling can also be used uncooked.)

Knead the dough again and divide into 8 portions. Roll each one into a small ball, then flatten. Add one portion of filling to each dough round and fold over to en-close it. Brush them with a little ghee and roll out on a floured surface, making triangular shapes.

Heat a griddle or heavy frying pan over a moderate heat; grease with 1 teaspoon ghee and place a parauntha on top. Apply 1 teaspoon ghee on top of the parauntha and cook for about 30 seconds. Turn over, apply another teaspoon of ghee and cook for 30 seconds. Turn over a couple of times, until dark brown spots appear on both sides. Remove and drain on absorbent kitchen paper. Make the other paraunthas in the same way and serve them hot.

Missi roti

Missi roti

•

| Preparation time 15 minutes | Cooking time 20 minutes | Serves 4 |

METRIC/IMPERIAL	AMERICAN
100g/4oz wholemeal flour	1 cup wholewheat flour
100g/4oz gram flour (besan)	1 cup gram flour (besan)
100g/4oz spinach or fenugreek leaves, coarsely ground	¼lb spinach or fenugreek leaves, coarsely ground
1 small onion, coarsely ground	1 small onion, ground
2 green chillies, coarsely ground	2 green chillies, ground
salt to taste	salt to taste
ghee, to serve	ghee, to serve

Place the flours, spinach, onion, chillies and salt to taste in a deep bowl. Add sufficient water to knead into a stiff dough. Leave to rest for 10 minutes and then knead again. Divide the dough into 8 portions. Roll out each one into a thick round, using a rolling pin.

Heat a griddle or heavy frying pan until very hot. Fry one round, turning over after about 10 seconds. Cook for about 25 seconds until brown spots appear all over. Although they are cooked like chapaatis, being a little thicker they will take a little longer to cook. Make the other breads in the same way.

Serve hot with a generous coating of ghee on one side. This bread goes well with a curry or dall.

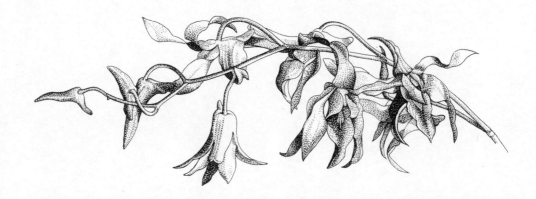

Deep fried bread

Puri

●

In India, these are served at any time of the day!
They are an integral part of a formal meal. Good for parties and picnics, too.

Preparation time 15 minutes   **Cooking time 20 minutes**   **Serves 4**

METRIC/IMPERIAL	AMERICAN
450g/1lb chapaati flour	4 cups chapaati flour
ghee as necessary	ghee as necessary

Place the flour in a bowl and rub in 1 teaspoon ghee. Add sufficient water to knead into a stiff dough. Divide into 16 portions. Roll each one into a ball and flatten it with the greased palms of your hands. Using a rolling pin, roll out each puri to about a 5cm/2-inch round. Cover with a damp cloth.

Heat sufficient ghee for deep frying to near smoking point in a *kadhai* or deep fryer. Fry the puris, 4 at a time, immediately turning over with a flat perforated spoon and pressing the puri so that it puffs up. Cook until golden brown all over. Remove and drain on absorbent kitchen paper. Serve hot with a curry. Note puris can be stored in an airtight container. They will still be nice and soft.

Puri stuffed with potatoes

Aalu ki kachauri

•

These are an elegant variety of Indian bread, usually served at a feast.
Serve them with dried or curried vegetables, pickles and poppadums.

Preparation time 20 minutes	Cooking time 20 minutes	Serves 4

METRIC/IMPERIAL	AMERICAN
225g/9oz plain flour	2 cups all-purpose flour
salt to taste	salt to taste
ghee as necessary	ghee as necessary
2 large potatoes, boiled, peeled and mashed	2 large potatoes, boiled, peeled and mashed
½ teaspoon garam masala	½ teaspoon garam masala
1 green chilli, finely chopped	1 green chilli, finely chopped
¼ teaspoon grated fresh ginger root	¼ teaspoon grated fresh ginger root
large pinch of red chilli powder	large dash of red chilli powder
½ teaspoon mango powder	½ teaspoon mango powder
1 tablespoon chopped coriander leaves	1 tablespoon chopped coriander leaves

Place the flour and a pinch of salt in a bowl and rub in 1 tablespoon ghee. Add sufficient water to knead into a stiff dough. Cover with a damp cloth.

Blend the potatoes, garam masala, chilli, ginger, chilli and mango powders and coriander together with salt to taste. The stuffing is now ready (it can also be lightly fried). Divide into 8 portions.

Knead the dough again and divide into 8 portions. Roll each one out into a ball and flatten it with the greased palms of your hands. Place one portion of filling on each round and roll up to enclose it completely. Dip into the ghee and roll out each puri to a 5cm/2-inch round.

Heat sufficient ghee for deep frying to near smoking point in a *kadhai* or deep fryer. Lower the heat and fry the puris, about 2 at a time. Cook for about 20 seconds on each side until they have puffed up and are golden brown all over. Remove and drain on absorbent kitchen paper. Serve hot.

Puri stuffed with peas

Matar bhari kachauri

Preparation time 15–20 minutes   **Cooking time 25 minutes**   **Serves 4**

METRIC/IMPERIAL	AMERICAN
175g/6oz plain flour	1½ cups all-purpose flour
salt to taste	salt to taste
ghee as necessary	ghee as necessary
1 teaspoon mustard seeds	1 teaspoon mustard seeds
½ teaspoon mango powder	½ teaspoon mango powder
2 green chillies, crushed	2 green chillies, crushed
1 teaspoon ground coriander leaves	1 teaspoon ground coriander leaves
½ teaspoon grated fresh ginger root	½ teaspoon grated fresh ginger root
½ teaspoon garam masala	½ teaspoon garam masala
175g/6oz peas, coarsely ground	1 cup peas, coarsely ground

Place the flour and pinch of salt in a bowl and rub in 1 teaspoon ghee. Add sufficient water to knead into a stiff dough. Cover with a damp cloth.

Heat 1 tablespoon ghee in a frying pan and fry the mustard, mango powder, chillies, coriander, ginger and salt to taste for about 1 minute. Stir in the garam masala and peas and cook over a moderate heat for another 5 minutes. Cool and divide into 8 portions.

Knead the dough again and divide into 8 portions. Roll each one into a ball and flatten it with the greased palms of your hands. Place one portion of filling on each round and roll up to enclose it completely. Roll each puri out to about a 5cm/2-inch round.

Heat sufficient ghee for deep frying to near smoking point in a *kadhai* or deep fryer. Lower the heat and fry the puris, 2 at a time. Cook for about 20 seconds on each side until golden brown all over. Remove and drain on absorbent kitchen paper. Serve hot with a dry or curried dish.

SAVOURY SNACKS
NAMKEEN PAKWAAN

Indian cookery seems to have an inexhaustible store of savoury snacks. The snacks come in many varieties and can be heavy or light on the stomach. A good many of them are suitable for starters, 'elevenses', as side dishes, to serve with tea or drinks, or taken on picnics. The most outstanding savouries are perhaps the pakodas, like the onion bhaaji, the samosas, the various kebabs and spiced chicken drumsticks.

The making of these snacks is often quick and straightforward. As a general rule, they offer considerable scope for experimentation, specially to those who have practised a few of the recipes 'by the book' first.

However delicious and tasty your concoction may be, unless it looks fetching people may not be attracted to it. Proper presentation will therefore make all the difference. Garnishing, for this reason, assumes a lot of importance for most snacks. The usual garnishing ingredients are green chillies, fresh coriander leaves, or lemon, tomato, onion and hard-boiled eggs, attractively sliced. Parsley is a useful substitute for coriander leaves.

Pakodas
Pakode

This dish is known by many names, like bhaaji, bhajji, bhujia, phulori, pakodi, pakoda, and equates roughly to its western cousin, the fritter. They can be served as starters, side dishes or snacks, and go down admirably with tea, Indian drinks and apéritifs. Pakodas can be both vegetarian or non-vegetarian and offer tremendous scope for experimentation, once you have mastered cooking them.

Spinach pakodas

Paalak ke pakode

Other leafy vegetables like yam, fenugreek or spinach leaves, can also be used in the same way, with equally tasty results.

Preparation time 10 minutes   **Cooking time 15 minutes**   **Serves 4**

METRIC/IMPERIAL	AMERICAN
225g/8oz gram flour (*besan*)	2 cups gram flour (*besan*)
300ml/½ pint water	1¼ cups water
salt to taste	salt to taste
1 teaspoon red chilli powder	1 teaspoon red chilli powder
1 clove garlic, crushed (optional)	1 clove garlic, crushed (optional)
225g/8oz spinach leaves	½lb spinach leaves
oil for deep frying	oil for deep frying

Put the flour, salt, chilli powder and garlic in a bowl and gradually whisk in the water to make a smooth, fluffy batter.

Heat the oil in a *kadhai* or deep fryer. Dip the spinach leaves well into the batter and fry, a few at a time, until they are nicely browned all over. Remove and drain on absorbent kitchen paper. Serve hot or cold, with a chutney of your choice. (For photograph see page 44.)

Onion bhaaji
Pyaazi pakodi

•

This is one of the best known Indian savouries in the West. Adjust the chilli content to your level of acceptance, by all means. When you feel confident, you may experiment by substituting a different vegetable, such as cauliflower.

Preparation time 15 minutes	Cooking time 20 minutes	Serves 6

METRIC/IMPERIAL	AMERICAN
225g/8oz gram flour *(besan)*	2 cups gram flour *(besan)*
pinch of bicarbonate of soda	dash of baking soda
300ml/½ pint water	1¼ cups water
1½ teaspoons salt	1½ teaspoons salt
4 green chillies, very finely chopped	4 green chillies, very finely chopped
oil for deep frying	oil for deep frying
225g/8oz onions, cut into rings	½lb onions, cut into rings

Put the flour, soda and salt in a bowl and gradually add the water to make smooth batter. Stir in the chillies and whisk thoroughly. Leave to stand for 10 minutes.

Heat the oil in a *kadhai* or deep fryer over a moderate heat. Dip the onion rings well into the batter and fry, a few at a time, until they are golden on both sides.

Remove and drain on absorbent paper. Serve the bhaajis hot with a chutney of your choice. (For photograph see page 29.)

Fish pakodas
Machhli ke pakode

Preparation time 10 minutes   **Cooking time 20 minutes**   **Serves 4**

METRIC/IMPERIAL	AMERICAN
2 large (size 1 or 2) eggs	2 large eggs
2 tablespoons lemon juice	3 tablespoons lemon juice
large pinch of salt	large dash of salt
pinch of red chilli powder	dash of red chilli powder
1 teaspoon chopped coriander leaves	1 teaspoon chopped coriander leaves
2 tablespoons cornflour	3 tablespoons cornstarch
ghee for deep frying	ghee for deep frying
4 fillets of white fish, steamed and cut into pieces	4 fillets of white fish, steamed and cut into pieces

Whisk the eggs, lemon juice, salt, chilli powder and coriander leaves together to make a batter. Add the cornflour and whisk thoroughly. Heat the ghee in a *kadhai* or deep fryer. Dip the fish pieces into the batter and fry until they are golden all over. Remove and drain on absorbent kitchen paper. Serve hot with a sweet of sour chutney or your choice.

Egg pakodas
Ande ke pakode

Preparation time 10 minutes   **Cooking time 15 minutes**   **Serves 4**

METRIC/IMPERIAL	AMERICAN
100g/4oz gram flour (*besan*)	1 cup gram flour (*besan*)
½ teaspoon salt	½ teaspoon salt
½ teaspoon red chilli powder	½ teaspoon red chilli powder
ghee for deep frying	ghee for deep frying
4 large (size 1 or 2) hard-boiled eggs, sliced	4 large hard-cooked eggs, sliced

Whisk the flour with sufficient water to make a medium consistency batter. Add the salt and chilli powder and whisk thoroughly. Heat the ghee in a *kadhai* or deep fryer. Dip the egg slices well into the batter and fry, a few at a time, until they are light brown on both sides. Remove and drain on absorbent kitchen paper. Serve hot with a sweet or sour chutney.

Samosas

Samose

Samosas are already well known in the West. I have known people travel fair distances to sample a few samosas! They have a superb taste and can be eaten hot or cold; ideal for serving with the tea or drinks, and for picnics and parties.

Samosas can be vegetarian as well as non-vegetarian. It is the filling that makes them different; other ingredients and methods are identical for samosas of either category. I have given a basic recipe for the outer pastry covering, which will provide for 12 samosa shapes, and a few recipes for the vegetarian and non-vegetarian fillings. Clearly, this dish also offers some scope for experimentation, according to your taste and liking.

Pastry

Ghee-daar aata

●

This recipe is for the basic samosa pastry.

Preparation time 15 minutes   Serves 6

METRIC/IMPERIAL	AMERICAN
225g/8oz plain flour	2 cups all-purpose flour
50g/2oz ghee	¼ cup ghee
pinch of bicarbonate of soda	dash of baking soda
½ teaspoon salt	½ teaspoon salt

Place the flour in a bowl and rub in the ghee. Add the soda and salt and continue rubbing in until the mixture becomes crumbly in texture. Add sufficient water to knead into a stiff dough and divide into 6 portions.

Flatten and roll out each portion into a thin round, cutting each in half to produce two half-moon shapes. Cover with a damp cloth and leave for 10–15 minutes, while the filling is being prepared. (For photograph of preparation of Samosas see page 45.)

Corn samosas

Bhutte ke samose

Preparation time 15 minutes   **Cooking time 25 minutes**   **Serves 6**

METRIC/IMPERIAL	AMERICAN
ghee as necessary	ghee as necessary
1 teaspoon mustard seeds	1 teaspoon mustard seeds
pinch of asafoetida powder	dash of asafoetida powder
1 teaspoon red chilli powder	1 teaspoon red chilli powder
100g/4oz fresh corn of the cob, boiled and crushed, *or*	¾ cup fresh whole kernel corn, boiled and crushed, *or*
100g/4oz drained, canned sweetcorn kernels, crushed	¾ cup drained, canned whole kernel corn, crushed
½ teaspoon grated fresh ginger root	½ teaspoon grated fresh ginger root
1 tablespoon lemon juice	1 tablespoon lemon juice
1 teaspoon salt	1 teaspoon salt
½ teaspoon garam masala	½ teaspoon garam masala
1 tablespoon chopped coriander or mint leaves	1 tablespoon chopped coriander or mint leaves
12 half-moon pastry shapes (see page 42)	12 half-moon pastry shapes (see page 42)
a little milk	a little milk

Heat 2 tablespoons ghee in a frying pan and fry the mustard seeds and asafoetida over a moderate heat for 2 minutes. Stir in the chilli powder, corn, ginger, lemon juice, salt and garam masala one by one, and cook for another 10 minutes. Sprinkle over the coriander and mix thoroughly. Leave to cool.

Take a piece of pastry, brush the edges with milk and fold it into a cone. Fill with 1 tablespoon of filling and seal the top. Make the other samosas in the same way.

Heat sufficient ghee for deep frying in a *kadhai* or deep fryer. Fry the samosas, 4–6 at a time, until they are golden brown all over. Remove and drain on absorbent kitchen paper. Serve hot or cold, with a sauce or chutney.

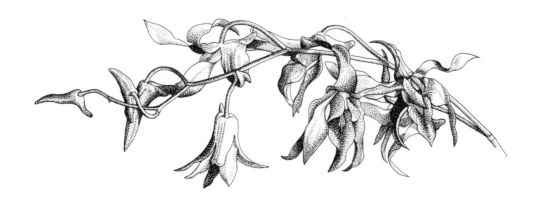

Chicken samosas

Murghi ke tikone

Preparation time 15 minutes   **Cooking time 25 minutes**   **Serves 6**

METRIC/IMPERIAL	AMERICAN
ghee as necessary	ghee as necessary
½ teaspoon white cumin seeds	½ teaspoon white cumin seeds
1 medium onion, chopped	1 medium onion, chopped
225g/8oz chicken, boiled, boned and chopped	½ lb chicken, boiled, boned and chopped
1 medium tomato, diced	1 medium tomato, diced
½ teaspoon garam masala	½ tablespoon garam masala
1 green chilli, chopped	1 green chilli, chopped
1 teaspoon salt	1 teaspoon salt
1 tablespoon lemon juice	1 teaspoon lemon juice
1 tablespoon chopped coriander leaves	1 tablespoon chopped coriander leaves
12 half-moon pastry shapes (see page 42)	12 half-moon pastry shapes (see page 42)
a little milk	a little milk

Heat 2 tablespoons ghee in a frying pan with the cumin seeds. Add the onion and fry until golden. Stir in the chicken, tomato, garam masala, chilli, salt and lemon juice, one by one, and cook over a low heat for 10–15 minutes. Add the coriander and mix thoroughly. Leave to cool.

Take a piece of pastry, brush the edges with milk and fold it into a cone. Fill with 1½ teaspoons chicken mixture and seal the top. Make the other samosas in the same way. Keep them covered with a damp cloth if making in advance.

Heat sufficient ghee for deep frying in a *kadhai* or deep fryer. Fry the samosas, a few at a time, until they are crisp and dark golden. Serve hot or cold, suitably garnished, with a chutney.

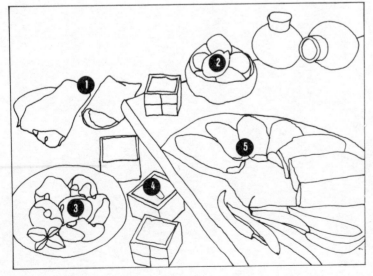

Right Carrot soup (see page 21)
Spinach pakoda (see page 39)

Overleaf Chaat dishes and South Indian specialities
1: Masala dosa (see page 66)
2: Flour wafers – golgappa (see page 61) 3: Dall dumplings in yoghurt (see page 62) 4: Cumin seed refresher (see page 106)
5: Aubergine chaat (see page 58)

Mixed vegetable samosas

Navratan samose

Preparation time 20 minutes   **Cooking time 25 minutes**   **Serves 6**

METRIC/IMPERIAL	AMERICAN
oil as necessary	oil as necessary
1 teaspoon white cumin seeds	1 teaspoon white cumin seeds
2 tablespoons chopped onion	3 tablespoons chopped onion
4 tablespoons diced, mixed vegetables, either fresh, tinned or frozen	5 tablespoons diced, mixed vegetables, either fresh, canned or frozen
½ teaspoon salt	½ teaspoon salt
1 green chilli, chopped	1 green chilli, chopped
½ teaspoon mango powder	½ teaspoon mango powder
½ teaspoon garam masala	½ teaspoon garam masala
1 tablespoon chopped coriander leaves or parsley	1 tablespoon chopped coriander leaves or parsley
12 half-moon pastry shapes (see page 42)	12 half-moon pastry shapes (see page 42)
a little milk	a little milk

Heat 1 tablespoon oil in a saucepan and fry the cumin and onion until golden. Stir in the mixed vegetables, salt, chilli, mango powder, garam masala and coriander. Cover and cook over a moderate heat for 10 minutes. Leave to cool.

Take a piece of pastry, brush the edges with milk and fold it into a cone. Fill with a heaped teaspoon of the filling and seal the top. Make the others in the same way.

Heat sufficient oil for deep frying in a *kadhai* or deep fryer. Fry the samosas, 4–6 at a time, until they are golden brown all over. When cooked to your satisfaction, remove and drain on absorbent kitchen paper. Serve hot or cold, with a chutney. (For photograph see opposite.)

Left Preparation of Mixed vegetable samosas (see above for recipe)

Minced meat samosas

Keeme ke samose

•

Any meat, such as beef, lamb, mutton or pork, can be used,
so long as it is lean and finely minced.

Preparation time 15 minutes	Cooking time 25 minutes	Serves 6

METRIC/IMPERIAL	AMERICAN
ghee as necessary	ghee as necessary
4 tablespoons chopped onion	5 tablespoons chopped onion
1 clove garlic, chopped	1 clove garlic, chopped
225g/8oz minced meat	½lb ground meat
50g/2oz peas	⅓ cup green peas
1 teaspoon salt	1 teaspoon salt
1 teaspoon red chilli powder	1 teaspoon red chilli powder
1 tablespoon chopped coriander leaves	1 tablespoon chopped coriander leaves
½ teaspoon grated fresh ginger root	½ teaspoon grated fresh ginger root
1 teaspoon garam masala	1 teaspoon garam masala
12 half-moon pastry shapes (see page 42)	12 half-moon pastry shapes (see page 42)
a little milk	a little milk

Heat 1 tablespoon ghee in a saucepan and fry the onion and garlic until golden. Add the meat and peas and turn over a few times. Stir in the salt, chilli powder, coriander, ginger and garam masala. Cover and simmer over a moderate heat for about 10 minutes. Leave to cool.

Take a piece of pastry, brush the edges with milk and fold it into a cone. Fill with 1 heaped teaspoon of the filling and seal the top by pinching the edges of the pastry together. Make the others in the same way.

Heat sufficient ghee for deep frying in a *kadhai* or deep fryer. Fry the samosas, 4–6 at a time, until they are golden brown all over. Remove and drain on absorbent kitchen paper. Serve hot or cold, with a sauce or chutney.

Potato samosas

Aalu ke samose

•

This is the most commonly used recipe for a vegetarian samosa. Potato mash (see page 83) could be substituted for this diced potato filling.

Preparation time 15 minutes   **Cooking time 25 minutes**   **Serves 6**

METRIC/IMPERIAL	AMERICAN
oil as necessary	oil as necessary
½ medium onion, chopped	½ medium onion, chopped
1 teaspoon mustard seeds	1 teaspoon mustard seeds
pinch of asafoetida powder	dash of asafoetida powder
1 teaspoon salt	1 teaspoon salt
225g/8oz potatoes, diced	½lb potatoes, diced
75g/3oz peas	½ cup peas
½ teaspoon red chilli powder	½ teaspoon red chilli powder
½ teaspoon garam masala	½ teaspoon garam masala
12 half-moon pastry shapes (see page 42)	12 half-moon pastry shapes (see page 42)
a little milk	a little milk

Heat 1 tablespoon oil in a saucepan and fry the onion until golden. Stir in the mustard, asafoetida and salt. Add the potatoes, peas, chilli powder and garam masala. Cover and simmer over a moderate heat for about 10 minutes.

Take a piece of pastry, brush the edges with milk and fold it into a cone. Fill with 1½ teaspoons potato mixture and seal the top. Make the others in the same way.

Heat sufficient oil for deep frying in a *kadhai* or deep fryer. Fry the samosas, a few at a time, until they are golden brown all over. Remove and drain on absorbent kitchen paper. Serve hot or cold, with chutney.

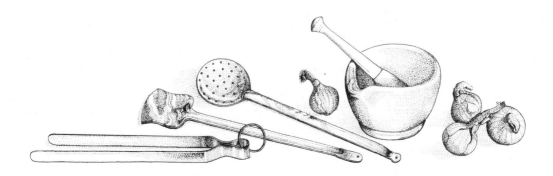

Kebabs, croquettes and cutlets
Kabab, tikia aur tikke

These dishes are very versatile. Apart from being admirable accompaniments to Indian drinks, they are favourites at parties or picnics. Serve them as snacks by themselves, or as side dishes with a main meal. Many of them can also be served as chaat dishes.

Like most other areas of Indian cuisine, these dishes can be both vegetarian and non-vegetarian.

Queen of hearts kebabs
Preeti raani kabab

Preparation time 25 minutes	Cooking time 20 minutes	Serves 4

METRIC/IMPERIAL	AMERICAN
450g/1lb minced lamb	1lb ground lamb
300ml/½ pint water	1¼ cups water
1 green chilli	1 green chilli
1cm/½-inch piece fresh ginger root	½-inch piece fresh ginger root
2 teaspoons salt	2 teaspoons salt
½ teaspoon garam masala	½ teaspoon garam masala
100g/4oz arrowroot	1 cup arrowroot
2 tablespoons chopped coriander leaves	3 tablespoons chopped coriander leaves
1 medium onion, chopped	1 medium onion, chopped
2 tablespoons satsuma segments, chopped	3 tablespoons satsuma segments, chopped
ghee for shallow frying	ghee for shallow frying

Place the lamb and water in a saucepan, bring to the boil and simmer until cooked and the water evaporates. Grind the lamb over a *sil-batta* or in a pestle and mortar with the green chilli, ginger, salt, garam masala and 2 tablespoons of the arrowroot. Then grind in half of the coriander, onion and satsuma. Mix thoroughly and divide into 8 portions. Make a small round of each.

Divide the remaining coriander, onion and satsuma mixture into 8 portions. Fill one portion into each of the lamb rounds. Roll them up and make thick rounds. Roll them over the remaining arrowroot. Heat the ghee on a griddle or in a heavy frying pan and fry the kebabs until they are brown all over.

Serve hot with a sweet or sour chutney of your choice.

Liver kebabs

Kaleji ke kabab

Preparation time 15 minutes   **Cooking time 25 minutes**   **Serves 4**

METRIC/IMPERIAL	AMERICAN
300ml/½ pint water	1¼ cups water
225g/8oz lamb's liver	½lb lamb's liver
2 tablespoons plain yoghurt	3 tablespoons plain yoghurt
1 small onion, chopped	1 small onion, chopped
½ teaspoon chopped fresh ginger root	½ teaspoon chopped fresh ginger root
1½ teaspoons salt	1½ teaspoons salt
½ teaspoon garam masala	½ teaspoon garam masala
1 green chilli, finely chopped	1 green chilli, finely chopped
1 tablespoon chopped coriander leaves	1 tablespoon chopped coriander leaves
rice flour for coating	rice flour for coating
ghee for deep frying	ghee for deep frying

Place the water, liver, yoghurt, onion, ginger and salt in a saucepan and cook over a moderate heat until the liver is tender and the water has evaporated (about 15 minutes). Remove from the heat, drain, and grind or liquidise into a mixture. Add the garam masala, chilli and coriander and mix well. Divide the mixture into 8 portions. Shape each into a thick round or long sausage. Roll the shapes in the rice flour.

Heat the ghee in a *kadhai* or deep fryer over a moderate heat. Fry the kebabs until golden all over. Remove and drain on absorbent kitchen paper.

Serve hot with a sweet or sour chutney.

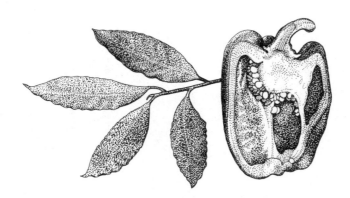

Quicky kebabs

Haazir huzoor

Preparation time 15 minutes plus standing time   Cooking time 20 minutes   Serves 6

METRIC/IMPERIAL	AMERICAN
450g/1lb finely minced beef	1lb finely ground beef
2 teaspoons salt	2 teaspoons salt
4 green chillies, finely chopped	4 green chillies, finely chopped
½ teaspoon grated fresh ginger root	½ teaspoon grated fresh ginger root
4 cloves garlic, chopped	4 cloves garlic, chopped
½ medium onion, finely chopped	½ medium onion, finely chopped
1 tablespoon chopped coriander leaves	1 tablespoon chopped coriander leaves
1 teaspoon garam masala	1 teaspoon garam masala
ghee for shallow frying	ghee for shallow frying

Place the meat in a large bowl, stir in the salt, green chillies, ginger, garlic, onion, coriander and garam masala and mix thoroughly. Leave to stand for about 20 minutes. Divide the mixture into 12 portions. Make sausage shapes of each.

Heat a little ghee on a griddle or in a heavy frying pan over a moderate heat. Fry the kebabs, a few at a time, until cooked. Serve hot, with garnishings and a chutney you prefer. (For photograph see page 29.)

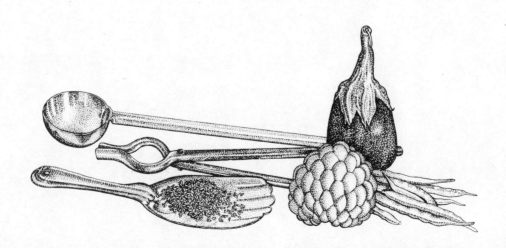

Indian fish croquettes

Bhaarti machhli tikka

Preparation time 20 minutes   **Cooking time 20 minutes**   **Serves 6**

METRIC/IMPERIAL	AMERICAN
450g/1lb white fish, boiled and mashed	1lb white fish, boiled and mashed
1 medium onion, finely chopped	1 medium onion, finely chopped
2 medium potatoes, boiled, peeled and mashed	2 medium potatoes, boiled, peeled and mashed
2 green chillies, finely chopped	2 green chillies, finely chopped
½ teaspoon grated fresh ginger root	½ teaspoon grated fresh ginger root
salt to taste	salt to taste
½ teaspoon ground black pepper	½ teaspoon ground black pepper
1 tablespoon chopped coriander leaves	1 tablespoon chopped coriander leaves
beaten egg and breadcrumbs for coating	beaten egg and breadcrumbs for coating
ghee for frying	ghee for frying

Mix the fish with the onion, potatoes, chillies, ginger, salt, pepper and coriander. Divide the mixture into 12 portions. Shape each portion into a triangle with the greased palms of your hands. Brush each triangle with the beaten egg and then roll over the breadcrumbs.

Heat a griddle or heavy frying pan and grease it with 1 teaspoon ghee. Fry the triangles, 4 at a time, for a couple of minutes. Turn over, add more ghee and fry until they are deep golden all over. Remove and drain on absorbent kitchen paper. Serve hot with garnishings and a chutney of your choice. (For photograph see page 29.)

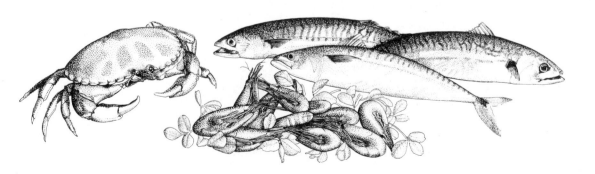

Eggs in minced meat

Nargisi kabab

●

This is a superior Mughal delicacy which can be deep fried or baked.

| Preparation time 15 minutes | Cooking time 20 minutes | Serves 6 |

METRIC/IMPERIAL	AMERICAN
225g/8oz minced meat of your choice	½lb ground meat of your choice
2 small onions, chopped	2 small onions, chopped
2 green chillies, chopped	2 green chillies, chopped
1cm/½-inch piece of fresh ginger root, finely chopped	½-inch piece of fresh ginger root, finely chopped
2 cloves garlic, chopped	2 cloves garlic, chopped
salt to taste	salt to taste
1 teaspoon cumin seeds	1 teaspoon cumin seeds
1 teaspoon garam masala	1 teaspoon garam masala
2 tablespoons gram flour *(besan)*	3 tablespoons gram flour *(besan)*
2 tablespoons chopped coriander leaves	3 tablespoons chopped coriander leaves
6 large (size 1 or 2) eggs, hard-boiled	6 large eggs, hard-cooked
ghee for deep frying	ghee for deep frying

Place the meat, onions, chillies, ginger and garlic in a saucepan and mix altogether. Cover and cook for 10 minutes. Remove from the heat and cool. Stir in the cumin seeds, garam masala, flour, salt and coriander and grind or mince them together. Thickly coat the hard-boiled eggs with this mixture.

Heat the ghee in a *kadhai* or deep fryer and fry the coated eggs until golden or well browned. Drain on absorbent kitchen paper. Serve hot with chutney.

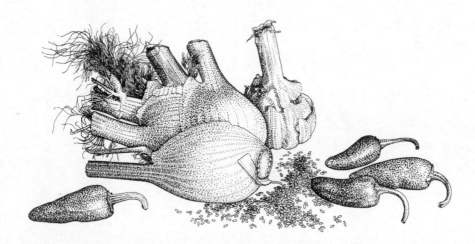

Fried chicken drumsticks

Chatpati murghi ki taangen

This dish is a great favourite of mine. In addition to deep frying, these drumsticks can also be baked or roasted.

Preparation time 20 minutes plus standing time   **Cooking time about 20 minutes**   **Serves 4**

METRIC/IMPERIAL	AMERICAN
8 chicken drumsticks, skinned	8 chicken drumsticks, skinned
8 tablespoons tandoori powder (see page 14)	9 tablespoons tandoori powder (see page 14)
2 tablespoons lemon juice	3 tablespoons lemon juice
salt to taste	salt to taste
4 large (size 1 or 2) eggs	4 large eggs
2 tablespoons cornflour	3 tablespoons cornstarch
breadcrumbs for coating	breadcrumbs for coating
oil for deep frying	oil for deep frying

Prick the drumsticks all over with a fork. Place them in a saucepan of salted water and simmer for 10 minutes. Remove and cool. Meanwhile, make a paste with the tandoori powder, lemon juice and salt. Smear this paste generously all over the chicken legs. Leave for about 20 minutes.

In a bowl, beat the eggs with the cornflour. Dip each drumstick first in this batter and then roll over the breadcrumbs.

Heat the oil in a *kadhai* or deep fryer over a moderate heat. Fry the chicken legs until golden brown all over. Remove and drain on absorbent kitchen paper. Serve hot, with garnishings or chutney of your choice.

Banana cutlets

Kele ke kabab

Preparation time 15 minutes   Cooking time 20 minutes   Serves 6

METRIC/IMPERIAL	AMERICAN
4 green bananas	4 green bananas
450g/1lb potatoes, boiled and peeled	1lb potatoes, boiled and peeled
2 tablespoons gram flour (besan)	3 tablespoons gram flour (besan)
2 teaspoons salt	2 teaspoons salt
2 green chillies, chopped	2 green chillies, chopped
½ teaspoon grated fresh ginger root	½ teaspoon grated fresh ginger root
2 tablespoons chopped coriander leaves	3 tablespoons chopped coriander leaves
pinch of bicarbonate of soda	dash of baking soda
ghee for shallow frying	ghee for shallow frying

Place the bananas in a saucepan of water, bring to the boil and simmer for 10–15 minutes. Peel and mash the bananas with the potatoes. Add the flour, salt, chillies, ginger, coriander and soda and blend thoroughly. You can make 12–18 banana shapes from the mixture.

Heat the ghee on a griddle or in a heavy frying pan. Fry the shapes, 3–4 at a time, until golden or well browned. Remove and drain on absorbent kitchen paper. Serve hot with a chutney of your choice.

Stuffed eggs

Bharwaan ande

Preparation time 20 minutes   Cooking time 25 minutes   Serves 4

METRIC/IMPERIAL	AMERICAN
1 tablespoon ghee	1 tablespoon ghee
1 tablespoon chopped onion	1 tablespoon chopped onion
2 tablespoons cooked minced meat	3 tablespoons cooked ground meat
salt to taste	salt to taste
1 green chilli, chopped	1 green chilli, chopped
1 tablespoon chopped coriander leaves	1 tablespoon chopped coriander leaves
½ teaspoon grated fresh ginger root	½ teaspoon grated fresh ginger root
1 tablespoon tomato purée	1 tablespoon tomato paste
large squeeze of lemon	large squeeze of lemon
4 large (size 1 or 2) eggs, hard-boiled	4 large eggs, hard-cooked
1 tablespoon cornflour	1 tablespoon cornstarch
1 large (size 1 or 2) egg, beaten	1 large egg, beaten
breadcrumbs for coating	breadcrumbs for coating
oil for deep frying	oil for deep frying
12 pieces of fried liver, to garnish	12 pieces of fried liver, to garnish

Heat the ghee in a frying pan and fry the onion until golden. Add the meat, salt, chilli, coriander, ginger, tomato purée and lemon and fry for 5 minutes. Cut the hard-boiled eggs into half, lengthways. Take out the yolks and add to the frying mixture. Cook for another 5 minutes and then remove from the heat and leave to cool.

Stir the cornflour into the beaten egg, making a batter. Place the breadcrumbs on a flat dish. Fill the meat mixture into the yolk cavity of each egg half, cover with another half to make complete egg shapes. Dip the stuffed eggs into the batter and then roll over the breadcrumbs.

Heat the oil in a *kadhai* or deep fryer over a moderate heat. Fry the eggs until they are golden brown all over. Remove and drain on absorbent kitchen paper. Serve, garnished with the fried liver, with a favourite chutney.

CHAAT AND SOUTH INDIAN DISHES
CHAAT KE MAZE AUR DAKSHIN BHARAT KE VYANJAN

In India chaat dishes are served as snacks in the evening and are extremely popular. They are used as starters, snacks and sometimes side dishes in the West.

A chaat shop usually opens to customers early in the evening and is well stocked with the main goodies and the chaat spices ie. salt, pounded or ground red chillies, garam masala, black salt and ground roasted cumin. There will also be an adequate supply of tamarind sauce (available here in bottles) as well as a mixture of yoghurt whisked with a little water.

There is a long list of dishes included in the chaat repertoire; the list varies from region to region. I have included the most well-known dishes here to give you an idea. I hope that you will enjoy making and eating these dishes with your family and friends.

This snack section would be incomplete if I did not include some delicious South Indian snacks. Rice, coconut, tamarind and mustard are the commonly used ingredients in the preparation of these dishes, some of which are already very popular in the West.

Dried peas chaat
Matar chaat

This is one of the main chaat dishes, served with the usual chaat ingredients and spices (see above). Crumble a few flour wafers (see page 61) over it, if desired.

Preparation time 5 minutes plus soaking time   **Cooking time 20 minutes**   **Serves 6**

METRIC/IMPERIAL	AMERICAN
225g/8oz dried whole peas, pre-soaked	2 cups dried whole peas, pre-soaked
½ teaspoon bicarbonate of soda	½ teaspoon baking soda
pinch of asafoetida powder	dash of asafoetida powder
chutneys and chaat spices, to serve	chutneys and chaat spices, to serve

Place the dried peas in a saucepan and add sufficient water to cover them. Stir in the soda and asafoetida powder and cook over a moderate heat for about 15 minutes until the peas are tender. Drain and serve as above.

Potato chaat

Kachaalu

Preparation time 10 minutes   Serves 4

METRIC/IMPERIAL	AMERICAN
450g/1lb potatoes, boiled and peeled	1lb potatoes, boiled and peeled
1 teaspoon salt	1 teaspoon salt
1 teaspoon black salt	1 teaspoon black salt
1 teaspoon red chilli powder	1 teaspoon red chilli powder
1 teaspoon white cumin seeds, dry roasted and ground	1 teaspoon white cumin seeds, dry roasted and ground
4 tablespoons lemon juice	⅓ cup lemon juice

Slice the cooked potatoes. Sprinkle a little salt, black salt, chilli powder and cumin on each serving and squeeze some lemon juice over the top. Eat with cocktail sticks.

Instead of lemon juice, you could use the normal chaat chutneys – sweet, sour or sweet-and-sour tamarind sauce and whisked plain yoghurt and water.

Fried peas

Tali hari matar

●

This is a versatile chaat dish and a favourite of mine. For variety, you may crumble a poppadum (see page 25), or a few flour wafers (see page 61) over just before serving.

Preparation time 10 minutes   Cooking time 20 minutes   Serves 4

METRIC/IMPERIAL	AMERICAN
1 tablespoon ghee	1 tablespoon ghee
2 cloves garlic, chopped	2 cloves garlic, chopped
350g/12oz peas	2 cups peas
1 green chilli, finely chopped	1 green chilli, finely chopped
1 teaspoon salt	1 teaspoon salt
1 tablespoon lemon juice	1 tablespoon lemon juice
1 tablespoon chopped coriander leaves	1 tablespoon chopped coriander leaves

Heat the ghee in a frying pan and fry the garlic until golden. Add the peas, chilli and salt. Cover and cook over a moderate heat for about 15 minutes, stirring once or twice during cooking.

When all the moisture has evaporated, stir in the lemon juice, sprinkle with coriander and serve hot.

Aubergine chaat
Baignee

Preparation time 10 minutes   **Cooking time about 10 minutes**   **Serves 4**

METRIC/IMPERIAL	AMERICAN
225g/8oz gram flour (*besan*)	2 cups gram flour (*besan*)
450ml/¾ pint water	2 cups water
50g/2oz mixture of rice flour and black bean (*urad daal*) powder	½ cup mixture of rice flour and black bean (*urad daal*) powder
2 aubergines, sliced lengthways	2 eggplants, sliced lengthways
oil for deep frying	oil for deep frying
chutneys and chaat spices, to serve	chutneys and chaat spices, to serve

Mix the flour, rice flour and *urad dall* powder together and gradually add the water stirring together carefully to make a batter. Dip the aubergine slices in the batter.

Heat the oil in a *kadhai* or deep fryer over a moderate heat. Fry the aubergine slices, 5–6 at a time, until they are golden brown all over. Remove and drain on absorbent kitchen paper. Add the chutneys and spices of your choice to each serving. Eat with your fingers while still hot. (For photograph see page 44.)

Potato in green coriander
Hari dhania ke aalu

Preparation time 15–20 minutes   **Serves 4**

METRIC/IMPERIAL	AMERICAN
450g/1lb small potatoes, boiled and peeled	1lb small potatoes, boiled and peeled
4 tablespoons coriander leaves	5 tablespoons coriander leaves
1 teaspoon salt	1 teaspoon salt
4 green chillies	4 green chillies
6 tablespoons lemon juice	½ cup lemon juice

Prick the potatoes all over with a cocktail stick, making sure you do not break them.

Grind the coriander leaves, salt, chillies and lemon juice together to make a thin paste. Smear this paste thickly over the potatoes and leave them for 2 minutes to soak in the paste. Eat with cocktail sticks; topping with chaat chutneys for variety.

Puffed rice chaat

Bhelpuri

This light chaat dish comes from the west coast of India.

Preparation time 15–20 minutes   Serves 4

METRIC/IMPERIAL	AMERICAN
25g/1oz puffed rice *(layya)*	1oz puffed rice *(layya)*
2 medium potatoes, boiled, peeled and diced	2 medium potatoes, boiled, peeled and diced
1 green chilli, chopped	1 green chilli, chopped
½ medium onion, chopped	½ medium onion, chopped
25g/1oz thin sevs (see page 133)	1oz thin sevs (see page 133)
4 tablespoons chopped coriander leaves	4 tablespoons chopped coriander leaves
2 teaspoons salt or to taste	2 teaspoons salt or to taste
4 tablespoons tamarind sauce	⅓ cup tamarind sauce
1 teaspoon red chilli powder	1 teaspoon red chilli powder
8 flour wafers (see page 61), unpuffed ones	8 flour wafers (see page 61), unpuffed ones

Soak the rice in warm water for about 10 minutes and then squeeze out the water. Mix in the potatoes, chilli, onion, sevs, coriander and salt. Stir in the tamarind sauce and chilli powder. Sprinkle the crushed wafers over the chaat and mix thoroughly. Serve immediately, as if left the puffed rice will go soggy.

Note: If bottled concentrated tamarind sauce is unavailable, substitute tamarind chutney (see page 109), omitting the salt and chilli powder.

Potato chops

Aalu ki tikiya

•

A large griddle with sizzling potato chops on it is a feature of most good chaat shops in India.

Preparation time 15 minutes	Cooking time 20 minutes	Serves 4

METRIC/IMPERIAL	AMERICAN
450g/1lb potatoes boiled, peeled and mashed	1lb potatoes, boiled, peeled and mashed
1 teaspoon salt or to taste	1 teaspoon salt or to taste
½ teaspoon garam masala	½ teaspoon garam masala
1 tablespoon coarsely chopped coriander leaves	1 tablespoon coarsely chopped coriander leaves
1 small onion, finely chopped	1 small onion, finely chopped
2 green chillies, chopped	2 green chillies, chopped
½ teaspoon grated fresh ginger root	½ teaspoon grated fresh ginger root
ghee for frying	ghee for frying
chaat spices and chutneys, to serve	chaat spices and chutneys, to serve

Mix the potatoes, salt, garam masala, coriander, onion, chillies and ginger together. Divide the mixture into 8 portions. Shape each portion into a thick round. Heat a little ghee on a griddle or in a heavy frying pan. Fry the potato chops for about 8 minutes, in 2 batches, until golden on both sides. Sprinkle with spices and serve with chutneys of your choice.

Note: the more seasoned chaat eaters normally have their chops sliced in half and fried again in some more ghee before being served.

Right World Peace Pullao (see page 76)

Translucent flour wafers

Golgappa or paani-puri

•

One of the most popular chaat dishes, you could eat many and still want more!

Preparation time 15 minutes   **Cooking time 15 minutes**   **Serves 4**

METRIC/IMPERIAL	AMERICAN
25g/1oz black bean (*urad daal*) powder	¼ cup black bean (*urad daal*) powder
100g/4oz plain flour	1 cup all-purpose flour
50g/2oz semolina	⅓ cup semolina
1 teaspoon melted ghee	1 teaspoon melted ghee
oil for deep frying	oil for deep frying
cooked or tinned chick peas for filling	cooked or canned chick peas for filling
cumin seeds refresher (see page 106)	cumin seeds refresher (see page 106)
chaat spices	chaat spices

Mix the flours, semolina, ghee and sufficient water to knead into a stiff dough. Roll out the dough into a thin round, then cut out 2.5cm/1-inch rounds (use a bottle screw cap). Cover with a damp cloth.

Heat the oil in a *kadhai* or deep fryer over a moderate heat. Fry the rounds, a few at a time, until they are puffed up and light brown all over. The puffing process is helped by placing a spatula or *karchhi* in the middle of the pan and moving it gently to make waves in the oil. When cooked, place, with great care, on absorbent kitchen paper to drain.

Take one wafer, make a hole at the top with your finger and drop in a few chick peas. Fill with cumin, sprinkle with spices and eat quickly in one go – serve one at a time. These wafers are usually eaten cold. (For photographs see opposite and page 13.)

Left Flour wafers – golgappa (see above)
Chicken tango (see page 101)

Dall dumplings

Wada

•

This dish is versatile and can be eaten as a snack, a chaat dish or as a side dish with a main meal.

Preparation time 15 minutes   **Cooking time 15 minutes**   **Serves 6**

METRIC/IMPERIAL	AMERICAN
225g/8oz black bean (*urad dall*) powder	2 cups black bean (*urad dall*) powder
1 teaspoon grated fresh ginger root	1 teaspoon grated fresh ginger root
large pinch of asafoetida powder	large dash of asafoetida powder
1 tablespoon fennel seeds	1 tablespoon fennel seeds
½ teaspoon salt or to taste	½ teaspoon salt or to taste
1 green chilli, chopped	1 green chilli, chopped
½ teaspoon bicarbonate of soda	½ teaspoon baking soda
oil for deep frying	oil for deep frying

Mix the *urad dall* powder, ginger, asafoetida powder, fennel, salt, chilli, soda and sufficient water together to make a thick paste. Whisk thoroughly. Take 1 tablespoon of the paste, place on a clean and greased surface or plastic sheet and, with wet fingers, shape into a thick round. Make a hole in the centre. Use up all the paste to make these shapes.

Heat the oil in a *kadhai* or deep fryer. Fry the dumplings, 3–4 at a time, until they are golden. Remove and drain on absorbent kitchen paper. Serve hot or cold.

Note: If you soak them in water, then squeeze out the water and add whisked yoghurt and the usual chaat spices, you have dall dumplings in yoghurt, *dahi wada*. (For photograph see page 44.)

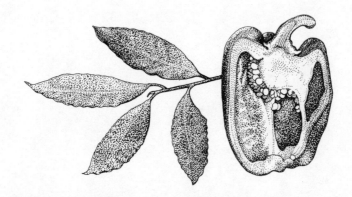

Khasta

Khasta

●

This one is the heavy-weight champion of chaat dishes – filling and satisfying.

Preparation time 20 minutes   **Cooking time 30 minutes**   **Serves 6**

METRIC/IMPERIAL	AMERICAN
Pastry:	*Pastry:*
450g/1lb plain flour	4 cups all-purpose flour
½ teaspoon salt	½ teaspoon salt
100g/4oz ghee	½ cup ghee
Stuffing:	*Stuffing:*
6 black peppercorns	6 black peppercorns
½ tablespoon coriander seeds	½ tablespoon coriander seeds
2 cloves	2 cloves
100g/4oz black bean (*urad dall*) powder	1 cup black bean (*urad dall*) powder
1 tablespoon chapaati flour	1 tablespoon chapaati flour
1 teaspoon bicarbonate of soda	1 teaspoon baking soda
1 tablespoon melted ghee	1 tablespoon melted ghee
1 tablespoon cumin seeds	1 tablespoon cumin seeds
oil for deep frying	oil for deep frying
2 medium potatoes, boiled, peeled and diced	2 medium potatoes, boiled, peeled and diced
To serve:	*To serve:*
tamarind sauce	tamarind sauce
whisked yoghurt	whipped yoghurt
chaat spices	chaat spices

For the pastry, mix the flour and salt together. Rub in the ghee and add sufficient water to knead into a stiff dough. Divide into 12 portions. Roll out and then flatten each one by hand into 5cm/2-inch rounds.

For the stuffing, coarsely grind the peppercorns, coriander seeds and cloves together. Add the dall, flour and soda and mix well. Add sufficient water to make a moist paste.

Heat the ghee in a *kadhai* or frying pan and fry the cumin for about 1 minute. Add the paste and stir thoroughly. Cook over a low heat for about 10 minutes. Leave to cool, then divide into 12 portions.

Take each pastry round, place a portion of stuffing on it, and completely enclose, rolling into a ball. Flatten with the hand and roll out a medium round – not too thin. Heat the oil in a *kadhai* or deep fryer and fry the khastas, 4 at a time, over a low heat, until they are light brown all over. Remove and drain on absorbent kitchen paper.

Make a hole on the top of each khasta and drop in some diced potato. Pour some tamarind sauce and yoghurt in and over the khastas and sprinkle with chaat spices. Serve 2 per person.

Fritters in tamarind sauce

Sonth pakodi

| Preparation time 15 minutes | Cooking time 15 minutes | Serves 6 |

METRIC/IMPERIAL	AMERICAN
450g/1lb gram flour (besan)	4 cups gram flour (besan)
300ml/½ pint water	1¼ cups water
½ teaspoon salt	½ teaspoon salt
1 green chilli, chopped	1 green chilli, chopped
pinch of bicarbonate of soda	dash of baking soda
oil for deep frying	oil for deep frying
To serve:	To serve:
tamarind sauce	tamarind sauce
whisked yoghurt	whipped yoghurt
chaat spices	chaat spices

Mix the flour and water together to make a thick batter. Add the salt, green chilli and soda and stir again.

Heat the oil in a *kadhai* or deep fryer over a moderate heat. Fry teaspoons of the batter, several at a time, and keep turning them over. Fry until golden brown. Remove and drain on absorbent paper.

Soak the fritters in warm water for 10 minutes. Then squeeze out the water and add the sauce, yoghurt and spices to each helping.

Note: If bottled concentrated tamarind sauce is unavailable, substitute with tamarind chutney (see page 109), omitting the salt and chilli powder.

Upma
Upma
•

*This is a kind of potato mash, sprinkled with green coriander, shaped in to balls and
eaten with saambhar sauce (see page 107)*

Preparation time 10 minutes   Cooking time 30 minutes   Serves 6

METRIC/IMPERIAL	AMERICAN
175g/6oz roasted semolina (see method below)	1 cup roasted semolina (see method below)
1 tablespoon ghee	1 tablespoon ghee
pinch of asafoetida powder	dash of asafoetida powder
½ teaspoon mustard seeds	½ teaspoon mustard seeds
4 medium potatoes, boiled, peeled and diced	4 medium potatoes, boiled, peeled and diced
1 teaspoon salt	1 teaspoon salt
2 green chillies, chopped	2 green chillies, chopped
1 tablespoon mixed dall powder	1 tablespoon mixed dall powder
300ml/½ pint warm water	1¼ cups warm water
1 teaspoon lemon juice	1 teaspoon lemon juice
2 tablespoons chopped coriander leaves	3 tablespoons chopped coriander leaves

Heat a griddle or heavy frying pan until hot and dry roast the semolina for 10 minutes.

Heat the ghee in a saucepan and fry the asafoetida and mustard. Add the semolina, potatoes, salt, chillies, dall powder and water and cook over a low heat for about 15 minutes, stirring. Add the lemon juice and blend well.

When the mixture is almost dry, remove from the heat, sprinkle with the coriander and make into small balls. Serve hot, to eat with saambhar sauce (see page 107).

Stuffed dosa

Masala dosa

●

This southern Indian delight has universal appeal and can be eaten with or without stuffing; the stuffing can be vegetarian or non-vegetarian. It is usually served hot with coconut chutney (see page 108) and saambhar sauce (see page 107)

Preparation time 20 minutes	Cooking time 30 minutes	Serves 6

METRIC/IMPERIAL	AMERICAN
Stuffing:	*Stuffing:*
1 tablespoon ghee	1 tablespoon ghee
1 teaspoon mustard seeds	1 teaspoon mustard seeds
½ teaspoon turmeric powder	½ teaspoon turmeric powder
1 large onion, chopped	1 large onion, chopped
225g/8oz potatoes, parboiled, peeled and diced	½lb potatoes, part cooked, peeled and diced
6 curry leaves	6 curry leaves
½ teaspoon salt or to taste	½ teaspoon salt or to taste
½ teaspoon red chilli powder	½ teaspoon red chilli powder
Dosa:	*Dosa:*
100g/4oz black bean *(urad dall)* powder	1 cup black bean *(urad dall)* powder
225g/8oz rice flour	2 cups rice flour
½ teaspoon bicarbonate of soda	½ teaspoon baking soda
½ teaspoon salt	½ teaspoon salt
oil for frying	oil for frying

For the stuffing, heat the ghee in a saucepan and add the mustard. Stir a few times before adding the turmeric, onion, potatoes and curry leaves. Sprinkle the salt and chilli powder over. Cover and simmer over a moderate heat for about 5 minutes until all the ingredients are well blended, stirring occasionally. Keep this stuffing warm.

For the dosa, mix the *urad dall* powder, rice flour and soda in a deep bowl. Add sufficient water to make a frothy batter of pouring consistency. Stir in the salt and mix thoroughly. Leave to stand for about 10 minutes. Heat a griddle or heavy frying pan to a high temperature over a moderate heat and drop ½ teaspoon oil on to it. Pour on 1 tablespoon of the batter and quickly spread it all round the griddle. Using a spatula, turn over and cook on the other side, making sure it does not burn. Serve at this stage, if stuffing is not required. This is known as plain dosa *(saada dosa)*.

While still on the griddle, place 2 tablespoons of the stuffing in a straight line down the centre of each dosa. Fold in the sides to close over the filling. Serve hot. (For photograph see page 44.)

RICE DISHES
CHAAWAL KI BAHAAR

Rice is very versatile and is the staple food of some 400 million people of India, living in Bengal, Bihar, parts of Uttar Pradesh and southern India. Dishes made from rice can be cheap and filling but they can also be sophisticated delicacies and Indians make a staggering range of rice dishes. It could be just plain boiled rice, to be served with a curry and accompaniments; or it could be rice and a dall boiled together like 'Rice and split green beans', which is easy to make and light on the stomach.

Alternatively, it could be the star attraction of the meal, namely, the pullaos and biriyanis. These dishes are superb and, being mild, should suit all palates and tastes. Many sweet dishes are made from rice, too!

The best rice dishes show each grain of rice separate, firm and fluffy with no hard centre; this requires care and attention. Also, in order to get best results you must always use good quality rice irrespective of whether you are making plain boiled rice or a plush pullao.

Plain boiled rice
Uble chaawal

Plain boiled rice is the staple diet of millions of people in India. It can be served with a vegetarian or non-vegetarian meal alike, but a curried dish should accompany it.

Preparation time 10 minutes   **Cooking time 15 minutes**   **Serves 4**

METRIC/IMPERIAL	AMERICAN
450g/1lb Basmati rice, pre-soaked	2 cups Basmati rice, pre-soaked
600ml/1 pint boiling water	2½ cups boiling water
100g/4oz ghee	½ cup ghee

Place the rice in a saucepan, add the boiling water and cook over a moderate heat until the rice is three-quarters cooked. Remove the pan from the heat and rinse the rice a couple of times under running hot water. Drain.

Heat the ghee in a saucepan and add the rice. Stir a few times, cover and leave over a low heat for about 5 minutes. Serve hot with a curry and side dishes or accompaniments of your choice. (For photograph see page 76.)

Potato, cauliflower and pea pullao

Aalu-gobhi-matar pullao

•

Here is a simple and mouth-watering pullao dish favoured by vegetarians throughout the world.

Preparation time 15 minutes   **Cooking time 30 minutes**   **Serves 4**

METRIC/IMPERIAL	AMERICAN
ghee as necessary	ghee as necessary
450g/1lb peas, small cauliflower and potato pieces	1lb peas, small cauliflower and potato pieces
1 medium onion, sliced	1 medium onion, sliced
4 cloves	4 cloves
2 bay leaves	2 bay leaves
8 black peppercorns	8 black peppercorns
1 teaspoon white cumin seeds	1 teaspoon white cumin seeds
1 brown cardamom	1 brown cardamom
2 (2.5-cm/1-inch) cinnamon sticks	2 (1-inch) cinnamon sticks
450g/1lb Basmati rice, pre-soaked	1lb Basmati rice, pre-soaked
1 teaspoon garam masala	1 teaspoon garam masala
600ml/1 pint warm water	2½ cups warm water
salt to taste	salt to taste
1 teaspoon red chilli powder	1 teaspoon red chilli powder

Heat sufficient ghee for deep frying in a *kadhai* or deep fryer. Fry the vegetables until golden. Drain on absorbent kitchen paper and set aside on a plate. (This ghee should not be used again in this recipe.)

Heat 50g/2oz/¼ cup ghee in a deep saucepan and fry the onion, cloves, bay leaves, peppercorns, cumin, cardamom and cinnamon together until golden brown. Add the rice and fried vegetables. Stir a few times, sprinkle with the garam masala and pour in the water and salt to taste. Cook for 10–15 minutes over a moderate heat until the rice is cooked.

Heat 1 tablespoon ghee for a few minutes and stir the chilli powder into it. Sprinkle this mixture over the pullao before serving.

Mushroom pullao

Guchchhi ka pullao

•

*This is an exotic vegetarian pullao which, being mild, can be enjoyed
by adults and children alike.*

Preparation time 15 minutes **Cooking time 30 minutes** **Serves 4**

METRIC/IMPERIAL	AMERICAN
ghee as necessary	ghee as necessary
225g/8oz black mushrooms, pre-soaked in hot water and diced, or use ordinary mushrooms	½lb black mushrooms, pre-soaked in hot water and diced, or use regular mushrooms
salt to taste	salt to taste
1 medium onion, finely chopped	1 medium onion, finely chopped
2 cloves garlic, chopped	2 cloves garlic, chopped
½ teaspoon grated fresh ginger root	½ teaspoon grated fresh ginger root
2 bay leaves	2 bay leaves
4 cloves	4 cloves
1 brown cardamom	1 brown cardamom
2 (2.5cm/1-inch) cinnamon sticks	2 (1-inch) cinnamon sticks
8 black peppercorns	8 black peppercorns
450g/1lb Basmati rice, pre-soaked	2 cups Basmati rice, pre-soaked
50g/2oz flaked almonds and cashews, lightly fried, to garnish	½ cup flaked almonds and cashews, lightly fried, to garnish

Heat 1 tablespoon ghee in a frying pan and fry the mushrooms for 1 minute over a moderate heat. Add 150ml/¼ pint/⅔ cup water, salt to taste, and cook for 5 minutes.

In a deep saucepan, heat 2 tablespoons ghee and fry the onion, garlic and ginger, together with the bay leaves, cloves, car- damom, cinnamon and peppercorns, un- til golden. Stir in the rice and 600ml/1 pint/2½ cups water with salt to taste. Bring to the boil and simmer until the rice is almost cooked. Add the mushrooms, cover and cook until the water is absorbed. Garnish with the fried nuts and serve hot.

Rice and split green beans

Moong ki khichdi

*This dish is moist and serves as a light meal. My mother always said, 'the four
ideal accompaniments of the* khichdi *dish are yoghurt, poppadums, ghee and pickles',
and she was absolutely right!*

Preparation time 10–15 minutes   Cooking time 20 minutes   Serves 4

METRIC/IMPERIAL	AMERICAN
ghee as necessary	ghee as necessary
pinch of asafoetida powder	dash of asafoetida powder
1 teaspoon white cumin seeds	1 teaspoon white cumin seeds
½ teaspoon red chilli powder	½ teaspoon red chilli powder
100g/4oz split green beans, skinless and pre-soaked	½ cup split green beans, skinless and pre-soaked
100g/4oz Basmati rice, pre-soaked	½ cup Basmati rice, pre-soaked
300ml/½ pint boiling water	1¼ cups boiling water
salt to taste	salt to taste
1 teaspoon turmeric powder	1 teaspoon turmeric powder
1 tablespoon chopped coriander leaves	1 tablespoon chopped coriander leaves

Heat 3 tablespoons ghee in a deep saucepan and fry the asafoetida powder, cumin and chilli powder for about 1 minute. Add the beans and rice and fry over a moderate heat for another 2–3 minutes. Pour in the water with salt to taste and the turmeric.

Half cover the pan and cook for about 15 minutes until the beans and rice are cooked and most of the water is absorbed. Serve hot with a generous sprinkling of coriander and ghee, together with desired accompaniments (see above).

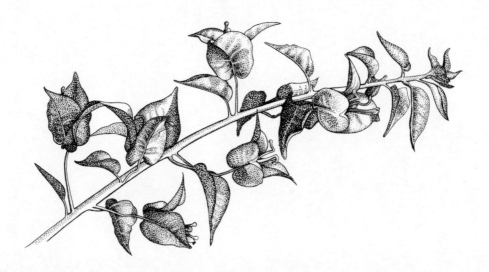

Fish biriyani

Machhli ki biriyani

Preparation time about 15 minutes   **Cooking time 25 minutes**   **Serves 4**

METRIC/IMPERIAL	AMERICAN
1 tablespoon plain yoghurt	1 tablespoon plain yoghurt
1 teaspoon mango powder	1 teaspoon mango powder
1 teaspoon garam masala	1 teaspoon garam masala
1 teaspoon red chilli powder	1 teaspoon red chilli powder
salt to taste	salt to taste
225g/8oz boneless fish pieces	½lb boneless fish pieces
ghee as necessary	ghee as necessary
1 medium onion, chopped	1 medium onion, chopped
2 cloves garlic, chopped	2 cloves garlic, chopped
450g/1lb Basmati rice, pre-soaked	2 cups Basmati rice, pre-soaked
8 whole green cardamoms	8 whole green cardamoms
1 brown cardamom	1 brown cardamom
2 (2.5cm/1-inch) cinnamon sticks	2 (1-inch) cinnamon sticks
1 teaspoon white cumin seeds	1 teaspoon white cumin seeds
2 tablespoons tomato purée	3 tablespoons tomato paste
600ml/1 pint water	2½ cups water
½ teaspoon saffron strands, steeped in 1 tablespoon kewda water	½ teaspoon saffron strands, steeped in 1 tablespoon kewda water

Make a paste with the yoghurt, mango powder, garam masala, half the chilli powder and salt to taste. Smear it over the fish pieces. Leave to stand for 10 minutes.

Heat 1 tablespoon ghee in a deep saucepan and fry the onion and garlic until golden. Add the rice, cardamoms, cinnamon, cumin, tomato purée and water and cook over a moderate heat for about 10 minutes until the water is absorbed.

Meanwhile, heat 1 tablespoon ghee in a pan and fry the fish until lightly browned. Stir the fried fish pieces into the rice over a low heat and sprinkle over the saffron mixture. Cover and cook for another 5 minutes. Serve hot by itself or with curry accompaniments, eg. salad, raita, chutney, pickles or poppadums.

Egg biriyani

Ande ki biriyani

Preparation time 20 minutes   **Cooking time 25 minutes**   **Serves 4**

METRIC/IMPERIAL	AMERICAN
100g/4oz ghee	½ cup ghee
1 large onion, finely chopped	1 large onion, finely chopped
2 cloves garlic, crushed	2 cloves garlic, crushed
2 bay leaves	2 bay leaves
2 (2.5cm/1-inch) cinnamon sticks	2 (1-inch) cinnamon sticks
1 brown cardamom	1 brown cardamom
4 green cardamom pods	4 green cardamom pods
8 large (size 1 or 2) eggs, hard-boiled	8 large eggs, hard-cooked
½ teaspoon turmeric powder	½ teaspoon turmeric powder
1 teaspoon red chilli powder	1 teaspoon red chilli powder
450g/1lb Basmati rice, pre-soaked	2 cups Basmati rice, pre-soaked
600ml/1 pint warm water	2½ cups warm water
salt to taste	salt to taste
1 teaspoon garam masala	1 teaspoon garam masala
To garnish	*To garnish*
4 tomatoes, thickly sliced	4 tomatoes, thickly sliced
1 tablespoon chopped coriander leaves	1 tablespoon chopped coriander leaves

Heat the ghee in a deep saucepan and fry the onion and garlic together with the bay leaves, cinnamon and cardamoms, until golden. Carefully pierce the eggs with a fork and add to the pan. Stir in the turmeric and chilli powders and fry for about 5 minutes. Add the rice and stir slowly and carefully for another 2 minutes. Pour in the water and salt to taste, and cook over a moderate heat for about 10 minutes until the rice is tender and the water is absorbed. Sprinkle the garam masala over the biriyani. Garnish with the tomato and coriander, and serve hot.

Mixed vegetable biriyani

Sabziyon ki biriyani

Preparation time 15 minutes   Cooking time 25 minutes   Serves 4

METRIC/IMPERIAL	AMERICAN
2 tablespoons ghee	3 tablespoons ghee
1 large onion, sliced	1 large onion, sliced
4 cloves garlic, chopped	4 cloves garlic, chopped
2 tablespoons tomato purée	3 tablespoons tomato paste
4 cloves	4 cloves
2 (2.5cm/1-inch) cinnamon sticks	2 (1-inch) cinnamon sticks
1 brown cardamom	1 brown cardamom
4 green cardamom pods	4 green cardamom pods
1 teaspoon garam masala	1 teaspoon garam masala
½ teaspoon turmeric powder	½ teaspoon turmeric powder
225g/8oz diced mixed vegetables, either fresh, frozen or tinned	½lb diced mixed vegetables, either fresh, frozen or canned
salt to taste	salt to taste
450g/1lb Basmati rice, pre-soaked	2 cups Basmati rice, pre-soaked
600ml/1 pint warm water	2½ cups warm water
1 tablespoon chopped coriander leaves	1 tablespoon chopped coriander leaves
50g/2oz almonds and cashews, chopped and lightly fried, to garnish	½ cup almonds and cashews, chopped and lightly fried, to garnish

Heat the ghee in a deep saucepan and fry the onion and garlic until golden. Stir in the purée, cloves, cinnamon, cardamom, garam masala and turmeric and simmer over a moderate heat for 2 minutes. Add the vegetables and salt to taste. Stir thoroughly and continue cooking for another 5 minutes. Add the rice, blend well and cook for a further 2–3 minutes. Pour in the water and cook for 10 minutes more, until the water is absorbed and the rice is cooked. Remove from the heat, sprinkle with the coriander and serve garnished with the nuts.

Chicken pullao
Murghi ka pullao

Preparation time 20 minutes   **Cooking time about 30 minutes**   **Serves 4**

METRIC/IMPERIAL	AMERICAN
450g/1lb small chicken pieces	1lb small chicken pieces
salt to taste	salt to taste
pinch of asafoetida powder	dash of asafoetida powder
large pinch of black cumin seeds	large dash of black cumin seeds
1 teaspoon garam masala	1 teaspoon garam masala
4 cloves	4 cloves
1 brown cardamom	1 brown cardamom
2 bay leaves	2 bay leaves
450g/1lb Basmati rice, pre-soaked	2 cups Basmati rice, pre-soaked
1 teaspoon red chilli powder	1 teaspoon red chilli powder
4 green cardamom pods	4 green cardamom pods
6 tablespoons ghee	7 tablespoons ghee
50g/2oz flaked almonds and cashews	½ cup flaked almonds and cashews
50g/2oz sultanas	⅓ cup golden raisins
2 tablespoons sliced onion	3 tablespoons sliced onion

Pierce the chicken pieces all over with a fork. Place in a deep saucepan and add sufficient water to come 1cm/½inch above the chicken. On a clean piece of muslin (or any clean, thin cloth), put a pinch each of salt, asafoetida and black cumin and also the garam masala, cloves, cardamom and bay leaves. Tie into a bag and drop into the saucepan. Place, uncovered, over a moderate heat for about 10 minutes until the chicken pieces change colour and begin to get tender. Stir in the rice and add 600ml/1 pint/2½ cups water together with salt to taste, chilli powder and

cardamom. Cook over a moderate heat for about 10 minutes until the rice is nearly cooked.

Heat 4 tablespoons ghee in a pan and fry the nuts and sultanas. When the sultanas begin to swell, scatter this mixture over the pullao. Cover the pan, lower the heat and cook for another 2 minutes (not forgetting to remove the spice bag before serving). Heat the remaining ghee and fry the onion until golden brown. Drain on absorbent kitchen paper. Sprinkle the fried onion over the pullao and serve hot. (For photograph see page 100.)

Minced lamb biriyani

Kofte ki biriyani

Preparation time 20 minutes   **Cooking time 30 minutes**   **Serves 4**

METRIC/IMPERIAL	AMERICAN
450g/1lb lamb, finely minced	1lb lamb, finely ground
½ teaspoon garam masala	½ teaspoon garam masala
½ teaspoon mango powder	½ teaspoon mango powder
1 tablespoon desiccated coconut	1 tablespoon shredded coconut
1 clove garlic, crushed	1 clove garlic, crushed
¼ teaspoon grated fresh ginger root	¼ teaspoon grated fresh ginger root
salt to taste	salt to taste
1 medium (size 3 or 4) egg, beaten	1 medium egg, beaten
ghee as necessary	ghee as necessary
pinch of asafoetida powder	dash of asafoetida powder
½ teaspoon black cumin seeds	½ teaspoon black cumin seeds
1 teaspoon red chilli powder	1 teaspoon red chilli powder
2 bay leaves	2 bay leaves
4 green cardamom pods	4 green cardamom pods
2 (2.5cm/1-inch) cinnamon sticks	2 (1-inch) cinnamon sticks
450g/1lb Basmati rice, pre-soaked	2 cups Basmati rice, pre-soaked
600ml/1 pint warm water	2½ cups warm water
½ teaspoon saffron strands, steeped in 1 tablespoon rose water	½ teaspoon saffron strands, steeped in 1 tablespoon rose water

Mix the lamb, garam masala, mango, coconut, garlic and ginger with a large pinch of salt. Bind the mixture with the egg and roll into small balls. Heat sufficient ghee for deep frying in a *kadhai* or deep fryer and fry the balls until golden brown. Remove and drain on absorbent kitchen paper and put on a plate.

Heat 1 tablespoon ghee in a saucepan and fry the asafoetida, cumin, chilli powder, bay leaves, cardamom and cinnamon over a moderate heat for 1 minute. Stir in the rice and fry for another 2–3 minutes. Pour in the water and salt to taste and simmer for 10 minutes until the rice is almost tender and the water absorbed.

Add the fried meat balls to the pan and carefully turn over the rice a few times. Lower the heat, cover the pan and cook for a further 5 minutes. Remove the pan from the heat, sprinkle the saffron mixture over the biriyani and serve hot.

World peace pullao

Shanti pullao

Preparation time 20 minutes   Cooking time 35 minutes   Serves 4

METRIC/IMPERIAL	AMERICAN
450g/1lb Basmati rice, pre-soaked	2 cups Basmati rice, pre-soaked
100g/4oz ghee	½ cup ghee
225g/8oz spring onions, roughly chopped	½lb scallions, roughly chopped
100g/4oz bacon, chopped	¼lb bacon, chopped
150ml/¼ pint peeled prawns	¾ cup shelled shrimps
225g/8oz pork, diced	½lb pork, diced
75g/3oz peas	½ cup peas
1 tablespoon tomato purée	1 tablespoon tomato paste
½ teaspoon ground black pepper	½ teaspoon ground black pepper
salt to taste	salt to taste
To garnish:	_To garnish:_
tomato slices	tomato slices
cucumber slices	cucumber slices

Place 600ml/1 pint/2½ cups water in a saucepan and bring to the boil. Add the rice and simmer over a moderate heat for about 5 minutes until the rice is partly cooked. Drain.

Heat the ghee in a deep saucepan and fry the pork for 15 minutes. Then add the onions, bacon and prawns and fry for another 5–10 minutes over a low heat. Stir in the rice and peas and mix thoroughly for 2 minutes.

Make a paste with the tomato purée, pepper, 150ml/¼ pint/⅔ cup water and salt to taste. Stir this paste into the rice, cover and cook over a low heat for about 10 minutes. Garnish with the tomato and cucumber. (For photograph see page 60.)

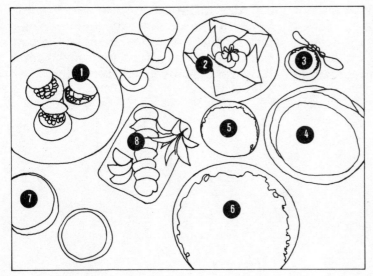

Right Fish dishes
Baked mackerel (see page 99)
Crab curry (see page 102)

Overleaf Vegetarian meal
1: Stuffed tomatoes (see page 87)
2: Samosas (see page 42)
3: Garlic chutney (see page 108)
4: Chapaati (see page 30) 5: Boiled rice (see page 67) 6: Peas and onion (see page 81) 7: Split green beans dall (see page 79)
8: Banana roundels (see page 113)

VEGETARIAN DISHES
SHAAKAAHAARI SABZIYAAN – SUKHI AUR RASEDAAR

India has long been an undisputed centre of vegetarianism in the world. These vegetarian dishes supply all the vitamins and proteins that the body requires.

The main category of dishes included in this section of the book are pulses, dry vegetable preparations, vegetable curries as well as 'whole' and stuffed vegetables. Most of these vegetarian dishes are accompaniments to a main meal but some also constitute main dishes in themselves.

Batter-drop curry
Boondi kadhi
•

This curry is best if the yoghurt is on the sour side, or use soured cream instead.

Preparation time 10 minutes   **Cooking time 20 minutes**   **Serves 4**

METRIC/IMPERIAL	AMERICAN
1 (142ml/5-fl oz) carton plain yoghurt	⅔ cup plain yoghurt
2 tablespoons gram flour *(besan)*	3 tablespoons gram flour *(besan)*
600ml/1 pint water	2½ cups water
6 tablespoons ghee	7 tablespoons ghee
2 teaspoons mustard seeds	2 teaspoons mustard seeds
pinch of asafoetida powder	dash of asafoetida powder
large pinch of turmeric powder	large dash of turmeric powder
1 teaspoon red chilli powder	1 teaspoon red chilli powder
salt to taste	salt to taste
50g/2oz batter-drops *(boondi)*	½ cup batter-drops *(boondi)*
1 tablespoon chopped onion	1 tablespoon chopped onion

Mix the yoghurt, gram flour and water together and whisk thoroughly, making sure no lumps form.

Heat half the ghee in a saucepan, add the mustard, asafoetida, turmeric and half the chilli powder and stir a few times. Pour in the yoghurt mixture and salt, bring to a boil and simmer for about 10 minutes. Add the *boondi* to the yoghurt mixture and cook over a moderate heat for another 5 minutes, stirring occasionally.

Heat the remaining ghee and fry the onion and remaining chilli powder for about 1 minute. Sprinkle over the curry. Serve hot with boiled rice or one of the breads. (For photograph see opposite.)

Left (from the top) Batter-drop curry (see above) Rain of nectar (see page 127) Cauliflower and potato dry vegetable curry (see page 85) Poppadums (see page 24)

Pigeon-pea purée

Toor (Arhar ki) dall

The pulse or dall dishes of India are legendary. Cheap to buy and simple to cook, they are popular for their food value and good flavour.

| Preparation time 15 minutes | Cooking time 40 minutes | Serves 4 |

METRIC/IMPERIAL	AMERICAN
100g/4oz melted butter	½ cup melted butter
1 medium onion, chopped	1 medium onion, chopped
2 cloves garlic, chopped	2 cloves garlic, chopped
1 teaspoon turmeric powder	1 teaspoon turmeric powder
225g/8oz pigeon peas *(toor dall)*	½lb pigeon peas *(toor dall)*
600ml/1 pint water	2½ cups water
salt to taste	salt to taste
1 teaspoon mango powder	1 teaspoon mango powder
1 teaspoon white cumin seeds	1 teaspoon white cumin seeds
½ teaspoon red chilli powder	½ teaspoon red chilli powder

Heat half the butter in a saucepan and fry half the onion and the garlic until golden. Stir in the turmeric and pigeon peas. Pour in the water, add salt to taste, bring to the boil and simmer for about 15 minutes. Lower the heat and continue cooking for another 10 minutes.

Stir in the mango powder and cook for a further 10 minutes, without stirring. Transfer the purée to a heated serving dish to keep warm.

Heat the remaining butter and fry the rest of the onion together with the cumin and chilli powder until golden brown. Add 1 teaspoon of this mixture to each serving of purée.

Split green beans dall

Chhili moong ki dall

•

*Indian pulses form an integral part of a vegetarian menu and have a universal appeal.
They are very simple and easy to cook.*

Preparation time 10 minutes   Cooking time 25 minutes   Serves 4

METRIC/IMPERIAL	AMERICAN
600ml/1 pint water	2½ cups water
225g/8oz skinless split green beans	½lb skinless split green beans
1 teaspoon turmeric powder	1 teaspoon turmeric powder
salt to taste	salt to taste
4 tomatoes, sliced	4 tomatoes, sliced
1 teaspoon garam masala	1 teaspoon garam masala
100g/4oz ghee	½ cup ghee
1 small onion, sliced	1 small onion, sliced
1 teaspoon white cumin seeds	1 teaspoon white cumin seeds
1 teaspoon red chilli powder	1 teaspoon red chilli powder

Place the water in a saucepan and bring to the boil. Lower the heat to moderate and stir in the split green beans, turmeric and salt to taste and cook for about 15 minutes. Add the tomatoes and garam masala and cook for another 5 minutes. Transfer to a heated serving dish.

Heat the ghee in a frying pan and fry the onion, cumin and chilli powder until deep golden, stirring well. Pour over the bean mixture. Serve hot with rice or chapaatis (For photograph see page 76.)

Turnip, potato and pea curry

Shaljum-aalu-matar

•

A main dish to be served with a rice dish or bread. The vegetables used here can be substituted according to personal preferences, such as carrots, cauliflower, tomato, yams, sweetcorn, pumpkin and aubergines.

Preparation time 10 minutes   **Cooking time 25 minutes**   **Serves 4**

METRIC/IMPERIAL	AMERICAN
100g/4oz ghee	½ cup ghee
225g/8oz turnip, cut into small pieces	½lb turnip, cut into small pieces
225g/8oz potatoes, cut into small pieces	½lb potatoes, cut into small pieces
75g/3oz peas	½ cup peas
1 teaspoon mustard seeds	1 teaspoon mustard seeds
salt to taste	salt to taste
½ teaspoon turmeric powder	½ teaspoon turmeric powder
1 teaspoon red chilli powder	1 teaspoon red chilli powder
600ml/1 pint water	2½ cups water
1 teaspoon garam masala	1 teaspoon garam masala
1 tablespoon chopped coriander leaves	1 tablespoon chopped coriander leaves

Heat half the ghee in a saucepan and fry the turnip, potatoes and peas for 5 minutes. Remove from the pan and put on one side.

Add the remaining ghee to the pan and fry the mustard seeds, salt, turmeric and chilli powder. Cover and cook over a moderate heat for 2 minutes.

Add the fried vegetables and water and cook for 15 minutes. Serve hot, sprinkled with the garam masala and coriander leaves.

Peas and onion

Matar do-piazza

•

This vegetable dish comes in between the moist and dry curried dishes.

Preparation time 15 minutes   **Cooking time 35 minutes**   **Serves 4**

METRIC/IMPERIAL	AMERICAN
100g/4oz ghee	½ cup ghee
5 large onions, thinly sliced, 1 onion to be reserved for garnish	5 large onions, thinly sliced, 1 onion to be reserved for garnish
2 bay leaves	2 bay leaves
1 brown cardamom	1 brown cardamom
6 black peppercorns	6 black peppercorns
175g/6oz peas	1 cup peas
2 green chillies, chopped	2 green chillies, chopped
2 medium tomatoes, quartered	2 medium tomatoes, quartered
1 teaspoon grated fresh ginger root	1 teaspoon shredded fresh ginger root
150ml/¼ pint plain yoghurt	⅔ cup plain yoghurt
300ml/½ pint warm water	1¼ cups warm water
1½ teaspoons salt or to taste	1½ teaspoons salt or to taste
1 teaspoon garam masala	1 teaspoon garam masala
1 tablespoon chopped coriander leaves	1 tablespoon chopped coriander leaves

Heat the ghee in a saucepan and fry one of the onions until golden. Drain the onion and reserve for garnishing.

Add the bay leaves, cardamom and peppercorns to the ghee in the pan and stir a few times. Keep the pan over a low heat. Add the peas, chillies, tomatoes, grated ginger and remaining onions and stir thoroughly for about 5 minutes. Pour in the yoghurt, water and salt. Cover, increase the heat to moderate, and cook for about 20 minutes. Sprinkle with the reserved fried onion, garam masala and coriander. (For photograph see page 76.)

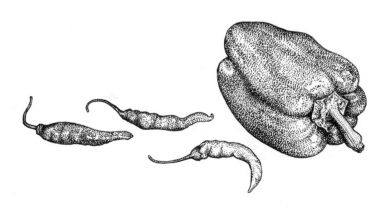

Cauliflower kofta curry

Gobhi ke kofte

Serve this curry as part of the main meal, with a rice dish or bread.

Preparation time 15 minutes   Cooking time about 30 minutes   Serves 4

METRIC/IMPERIAL	AMERICAN
225g/8oz cauliflower, grated	½lb cauliflower, grated
1 potato, grated	1 potato, grated
50g/2oz rice flour	½ cup rice flour
½ teaspoon salt	½ teaspoon salt
1 green chilli, chopped	1 green chilli, chopped
pinch of green cardamom powder	dash of green cardamom powder
1 large (size 1 or 2) egg, beaten	1 large egg, beaten
ghee for deep frying	ghee, for deep frying
300ml/½ pint gravy (see page 20)	1¼ cups gravy (see page 20)
1 teaspoon garam masala	1 teaspoon garam masala
1 tablespoon chopped coriander leaves	1 tablespoon chopped coriander leaves

Steam the cauliflower and potato in a steamer or covered colander over a pan of simmering water for about 2 minutes. Mix with the rice flour, salt, chilli, cardamom and beaten egg to make a dough. Break off small pieces and roll into balls.

Heat the ghee in a *kadhai* or deep fryer over a moderate heat and fry the balls (*koftas*) until they are golden brown all over. Remove and drain on absorbent kitchen paper.

Place the gravy in a saucepan and bring to the boil. Carefully drop in the koftas and cook over a moderate heat for about 5 minutes. Sprinkle with the garam masala and coriander. Serve hot.

Potato mash

Aalu ka bhurta

This potato mash is nothing like its namesake found in the West.

Preparation time 10 minutes   **Cooking time about 10 minutes**   **Serves 4**

METRIC/IMPERIAL	AMERICAN
1 teaspoon ghee	1 teaspoon ghee
½ teaspoon white cumin seeds	½ teaspoon white cumin seeds
pinch of asafoetida powder	dash of asafoetida powder
225g/8oz potatoes, boiled, peeled and mashed	½lb potatoes, boiled, peeled and mashed
salt to taste	salt to taste
½ teaspoon mango powder	½ teaspoon mango powder
1 green chilli, chopped	1 green chilli, chopped
pinch of grated fresh ginger root	dash of grated fresh ginger root
1 tablespoon chopped coriander leaves	1 tablespoon chopped coriander leaves

Heat the ghee to a high temperature in a *kadhai* or frying pan. Add the cumin and asafoetida and stir. Add the potatoes, salt, mango powder, chilli and ginger and cook for 2 minutes, stirring constantly. Sprinkle with coriander. Serve as a side dish.

Tomato mash

Tamaatar ka bhurta

Preparation time 10 minutes   **Cooking time 10 minutes**   **Serves 4**

METRIC/IMPERIAL	AMERICAN
1 teaspoon ghee	1 teaspoon ghee
1 small spring onion, finely chopped	1 small scallion, finely chopped
4 medium tomatoes, skinned	4 medium tomatoes, skinned
pinch of ground black pepper	dash of ground black pepper
½ teaspoon salt or to taste	½ teaspoon salt or to taste
1 green chilli, chopped	1 green chilli, chopped
pinch of garam masala	dash of garam masala
1 tablespoon coarsely chopped coriander leaves	1 tablespoon coarsely chopped coriander leaves

Heat the ghee in a frying pan and fry the onion. Add the tomatoes, pepper, salt, chilli and garam masala and mash together over the heat. Sprinkle with the coriander leaves and serve immediately as an accompaniment to a main meal.

Spinach and potato

Paalak aalu ki sukhi sabzi

Another popular dry vegetable dish.

Preparation time 10 minutes **Cooking time 15–20 minutes** **Serves 4**

METRIC/IMPERIAL	AMERICAN
1 tablespoon melted butter	1 tablespoon melted butter
pinch of asafoetida powder	dash of asafoetida powder
1 teaspoon white cumin seeds	1 teaspoon white cumin seeds
1kg/2lb spinach, chopped	2lb spinach, chopped
450g/1lb potatoes, quartered	1lb potatoes, quartered
salt to taste	salt to taste
2 green chillies, chopped	2 green chillies, chopped
To garnish:	*To garnish:*
tomato slices	tomato slices
lemon slices	lemon slices

Heat the butter in a saucepan and fry the asafoetida and cumin for 2 minutes. Add the spinach, potatoes, salt and chillies. Cover and cook over a moderate heat for about 10 minutes.

Stir several times and then arrange the tomato and lemon slices over the mixture. Cover, lowering the heat and cook for another 5 minutes. Serve hot as a side dish.

Cauliflower and potato dry vegetable
Gobhi aalu ki sukhi sabzi

•

This is a delicious side dish which adds piquancy to a bland meal! You can also serve it with puris or paraunthas (see pages 35–31).

Preparation time 10 minutes   Cooking time 20 minutes   Serves 4

METRIC/IMPERIAL	AMERICAN
2 tablespoons ghee	3 tablespoons ghee
1 large onion, chopped	1 large onion, chopped
225g/8oz cauliflower florets	½lb cauliflower florets
225g/8oz potatoes, cut into small pieces	½lb potatoes, cut into small pieces
2 large ripe tomatoes, sliced	2 large ripe tomatoes, sliced
salt to taste	salt to taste
2 green chillies, chopped	2 green chillies, chopped
2 cloves garlic, chopped	2 cloves garlic, chopped
½ teaspoon grated fresh ginger root	½ teaspoon grated fresh ginger root
1 teaspoon garam masala	1 teaspoon garam masala
1 tablespoon chopped coriander leaves	1 tablespoon chopped coriander leaves

Heat the ghee in a saucepan and fry the onion until golden. Add the cauliflower, potatoes, tomatoes, salt, chillies, garlic and grated ginger to the pan, one by one. Cover and cook over a moderate heat for about 15 minutes until the cauliflower and potato are tender, stirring occasionally.

Sprinkle over the garam masala and coriander. Serve hot. (For photograph see page 77.)

Stuffed okra

Bharwaan bhindi

Preparation time 15 minutes　　**Cooking time 20–25 minutes**　　**Serves 6**

METRIC/IMPERIAL	AMERICAN
450g/1lb okra (lady's fingers)	1lb okra
2 tablespoons aniseed	3 tablespoons aniseed
2 tablespoons coriander seeds	3 tablespoons coriander seeds
1 tablespoon white cumin seeds	1 tablespoon white cumin seeds
1 teaspoon turmeric powder	1 teaspoon turmeric powder
1 teaspoon red chilli powder	1 teaspoon red chilli powder
1 tablespoon mango powder	1 tablespoon mango powder
1 teaspoon salt, or to taste	1 teaspoon salt, or to taste
6 tablespoons oil	½ cup oil
1 teaspoon asafoetida powder	1 teaspoon asafoetida powder

Wash the okra, chop off the tops and slit them lengthways, without halving them. Remove the pulp and reserve.

Heat a griddle or heavy frying pan over a moderate heat and roast the aniseed, coriander and half the cumin seeds until they give off an aromatic smell. Grind them together. Add the turmeric, chilli and mango powders, salt and okra pulp.

Make a thick paste by adding half the oil. Stuff this paste into the okra.

Heat the remaining oil in a *kadhai* or frying pan. Fry the asafoetida and remaining cumin for 2 minutes. Carefully arrange the okra in the pan. Cook, uncovered, over a low heat for about 15 minutes until tender. Serve hot as a dry side dish. (For photograph see page 100.)

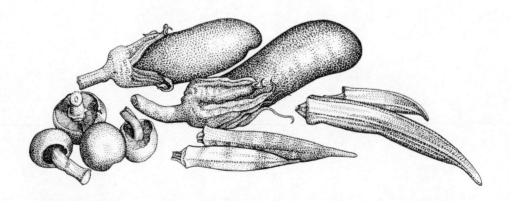

Stuffed tomatoes

Bharwaan tamaatar

●

*This superb-tasting dish can also be made with either a mixed vegetable or a minced
meat filling. It is an ideal side dish with a main meal.*

Preparation time 15 minutes   **Cooking time 25 minutes**   **Serves 4**

METRIC/IMPERIAL	AMERICAN
8 firm ripe tomatoes	8 firm ripe tomatoes
175g/6oz ghee	¾ cup ghee
1 medium onion, finely chopped	1 medium onion, finely chopped
1 clove garlic, finely chopped	1 clove garlic, finely chopped
225g/8oz potatoes, parboiled and diced	½lb potatoes, part cooked and diced
75g/3oz peas	½ cup peas
1 teaspoon salt, or to taste	1 teaspoon salt, or to taste
½ teaspoon garam masala	½ teaspoon garam masala
1 green chilli, chopped	1 green chilli, chopped
½ teaspoon grated fresh ginger root	½ teaspoon grated fresh ginger root
1 teaspoon white cumin seeds	1 teaspoon white cumin seeds
1 tablespoon chopped coriander leaves	1 tablespoon chopped coriander leaves

Slice the tops off the tomatoes and scoop out the pulp. Reserve the tops, to use as lids later.

Heat 50g/2oz/¼ cup of the ghee in a *kadhai* or frying pan. Fry the onion and garlic until golden. Stir in the potatoes, peas, salt, garam masala, chilli, ginger and tomato pulp. Cook over a low heat for about 5 minutes until almost tender. Divide the cooked mixture into 8 portions.

Fill each tomato with the mixture. Replace the tops and secure with wooden cocktail sticks.

Heat the remaining ghee in a shallow pan and fry the cumin for 2 minutes. Carefully arrange the tomatoes in the pan, on top of the cumin, cover and cook for about 10 minutes. Serve hot, sprinkled with the coriander. (For photograph see page 76.)

Stuffed potatoes

Bharwaan aalu

•

The filling used in this recipe is vegetarian but a non-vegetarian meat or fish filling can be used instead.

| **Preparation time 15 minutes** | **Cooking time about 25 minutes** | **Serves 4** |

METRIC/IMPERIAL	AMERICAN
8 medium potatoes, peeled	8 medium potatoes, peeled
2 cauliflower florets, chopped	2 cauliflower florets, chopped
1 green pepper, cored, seeded and chopped	1 green pepper, cored, seeded and chopped
1 tablespoon peas	1 tablespoon peas
1 tablespoon chopped onion	1 tablespoon chopped onion
2 green chillies, chopped	2 green chillies, chopped
2 cloves garlic, chopped	2 cloves garlic, chopped
1 teaspoon salt, or to taste	1 teaspoon salt, or to taste
150ml/¼ pint water	⅔ cup water
50g/2oz ghee	¼ cup ghee
4 medium tomatoes, quartered	4 medium tomatoes, quartered
1 tablespoon chopped coriander leaves	1 tablespoon chopped coriander leaves

Slice off the top from the potatoes – a thick enough slice to be used as a lid later – and carefully scoop out the inside.

Place the cauliflower, green pepper, peas, onion, chillies, garlic and half the salt in a saucepan with the water. Parboil until the water is fully absorbed into the mixture. Fill this mixture into the potatoes, cover with the potato lids and secure with wooden cocktail sticks.

Heat the ghee in a *kadhai* or saucepan and cook the tomatoes with the remaining salt over a moderate heat for 2 minutes. Carefully arrange the stuffed potatoes over the tomato mixture, cover tightly and cook the potatoes in their own steam for about 10 minutes until tender.

Sprinkle with the coriander. Serve as a side dish, or to eat with one of the Indian breads.

MEAT, POULTRY AND FISH
MAANSAAHAARI KHAANE

The population of India is roughly divided half and half between the vegetarians and non-vegetarians. The non-vegetarian side of Indian cuisine comprises many juicy, tender delicacies made with beef, pork, mutton, lamb, chicken, fish, etc.

Curries are of course the most famous of Indian dishes; they are prepared in many ways which produce different flavours and tastes. Besides curries, there is a wealth of kebabs and cutlets which can be served as snacks, accompaniments or main dishes. In fact, there is a great variety of meat, poultry and fish dishes in Indian cuisine.

Minced lamb curry
Keema shorwedaar

This is an ideal quick and easy non-vegetarian curry. It can be served with any rice dish or bread. Any meat of your choice can be used, as long as it is lean and finely minced.

Preparation time 15 minutes   **Cooking time 20 minutes**   **Serves 4**

METRIC/IMPERIAL	AMERICAN
3 tablespoons oil	¼ cup oil
1 large onion, finely chopped	1 large onion, finely chopped
1 teaspoon turmeric powder	1 teaspoon turmeric powder
1 teaspoon red chilli powder	1 teaspoon red chilli powder
450g/1lb lean lamb, minced	1lb lean lamb, ground
75g/3oz peas	½ cup peas
1 teaspoon grated fresh ginger root	1 teaspoon grated fresh ginger root
1 (142ml/5-fl oz) carton plain yoghurt	⅔ cup plain yoghurt
1½ teaspoons salt, or to taste	1½ teaspoons salt, or to taste
300ml/½ pint water	1¼ cups water
4 hard-boiled eggs, shelled	4 hard-cooked eggs, shelled
2 tomatoes, quartered	2 tomatoes, quartered
1 teaspoon garam masala	1 teaspoon garam masala
1 tablespoon chopped coriander leaves	1 tablespoon chopped coriander leaves

Heat the oil in a saucepan and fry the onion until golden. Stir in the turmeric and chilli powders, lamb, peas and ginger, one by one, and blend thoroughly. After stirring for about 2 minutes, add the yoghurt, salt and water and stir well. Add the eggs and tomatoes, cover and cook over a moderate heat for about 15 minutes. Serve hot, sprinkled with the garam masala and coriander.

Pork vindaloo

Shikaar vindaloo

•

This dish is normally hot and sour and comes from the south of India, where even the
mild curries are hotter than the hot ones of the North! Mustard oil, vinegar, tamarind
juice and desiccated coconut are always used in its preparation.
Serve with a cooling raita (see pages 103–105)

Preparation time 10 minutes   Cooking time 35–40 minutes   Serves 4

METRIC/IMPERIAL	AMERICAN
6 tablespoons mustard oil	½ cup mustard oil
1 medium onion, chopped	1 medium onion, chopped
4 cloves garlic, chopped	4 cloves garlic, chopped
1 tablespoon vindaloo powder	1 tablespoon vindaloo powder
2 teaspoons vinegar	2 teaspoons vinegar
450g/1lb lean pork, cut into small pieces	1lb lean pork, cut into small pieces
2 green chillies, chopped	2 green chillies, chopped
150ml/¼ pint water	⅔ cup water
2 teaspoons salt, or to taste	2 teaspoons salt, or to taste
1 tablespoon bottled tamarind juice	1 tablespoon bottled tamarind juice
1 tablespoon desiccated coconut	1 tablespoon shredded coconut

Heat the oil in a saucepan and fry the onion and garlic until golden. Make a paste with the vindaloo powder and vinegar and add to the pan. Cook, stirring, for 2 minutes. Pierce the pork well with a fork and add with the chillies to the pan and blend thoroughly. Pour in the water and salt. Cover and cook over a moderate heat for about 20 minutes.

Remove the lid and continue cooking. When all the water has evaporated, add the tamarind and cook for another 10 minutes. Serve hot, sprinkled with coconut. (For photograph see page 100.)

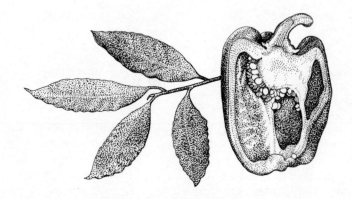

Nargisi kofta curry

Nargisi kofte

●

This superior Mughal dish can be served as a snack and, later, also curried up; in this way it resembles the foogath dishes (see page 94).

Preparation time about 10 minutes   **Cooking time 25 minutes**   **Serves 6**

METRIC/IMPERIAL	AMERICAN
3 tablespoons ghee	¼ cup ghee
2 small onions, finely chopped	2 small onions, finely chopped
2 cloves garlic, chopped	2 cloves garlic, chopped
4 large tomatoes, quartered	4 large tomatoes, quartered
½ teaspoon grated fresh ginger root	½ teaspoon grated fresh ginger root
½ teaspoon turmeric powder	½ teaspoon turmeric powder
½ teaspoon garam masala	½ teaspoon garam masala
1 brown cardamom	1 brown cardamom
2 bay leaves	2 bay leaves
2 (2.5cm/1-inch) cinnamon sticks	2 (1-inch) cinnamon sticks
½ teaspoon crushed coriander	½ teaspoon crushed coriander
1 teaspoon red chilli powder	1 teaspoon red chilli powder
2 tablespoons plain yoghurt	3 tablespoons plain yoghurt
salt to taste	salt to taste
300ml/½ pint water	1¼ cups water
6 eggs in minced meat, *nargisi kababs* (see page 52)	6 eggs in minced meat, *nargisi kababs* (see page 52)
1 tablespoon chopped coriander leaves, to garnish	1 tablespoon chopped coriander leaves, to garnish

Heat the ghee in a saucepan and fry the onions and garlic until golden. Add the tomatoes, ginger, turmeric, garam masala, cardamom, bay leaves, cinnamon, coriander and chilli powder and fry over a moderate heat for about 2 minutes, stirring constantly. Stir in the yoghurt, salt and water. Cover, bring to the boil and simmer for about 10 minutes.

Add the eggs in minced meat to the pan, cook for 5 minutes, then remove from the heat.

Garnish with the chopped coriander leaves before serving.

Beef kofta curry

Gosht ke kofte

Here is an offering from the kofta cooks of India, which is very quick and easy to make.

Preparation time 10–15 minutes   **Cooking time 30 minutes**   **Serves 4**

METRIC/IMPERIAL	AMERICAN
2 teaspoons salt	2 teaspoons salt
2 cloves garlic, crushed	2 cloves garlic, crushed
225g/8oz minced beef	½lb ground beef
2 tablespoons ghee	3 tablespoons ghee
4 cloves	4 cloves
8 black peppercorns	8 black peppercorns
2 (5cm/2-inch) cinnamon sticks	2 (2-inch) cinnamon sticks
2 bay leaves	2 bay leaves
1 brown cardamom	1 brown cardamom
1 medium onion, finely chopped	1 medium onion, finely chopped
2 tomatoes, quartered	2 tomatoes, quartered
1 tablespoon plain yoghurt	1 tablespoon plain yoghurt
½ teaspoon red chilli powder	½ teaspoon red chilli powder
300ml/½ pint water	1¼ cups water
½ teaspoon garam masala	½ teaspoon garam masala
1 tablespoon chopped coriander leaves	1 tablespoon chopped coriander leaves

Add ½ teaspoon of the salt and the garlic to the beef. Mix well and divide the mixture into 12 portions. Roll each portion into a ball.

Heat the ghee over a moderate heat in a deep saucepan. Stir in the cloves, peppercorns, cinnamon, bay leaves and cardamom, then the onion. When the onion is golden, add the tomatoes, yoghurt and chilli powder. Stir a few times. Pour in the water and the remaining salt and bring to the boil. Drop in the meat-balls.

Half cover the pan, bring the mixture to the boil and simmer for another 15 minutes. Serve hot, sprinkled with the garam masala and coriander.

Lamb Madras

Bhoona gosht

●

This is a 'hot' favourite from the south of India. You may adjust the quantities of chilli, to make it hotter or milder as you wish.

Preparation time 10 minutes   **Cooking time 30 minutes**   **Serves 4**

METRIC/IMPERIAL	AMERICAN
1 tablespoon mustard oil or ghee	1 tablespoon mustard oil or ghee
1 medium onion, finely chopped	1 medium onion, finely chopped
2 cloves garlic, sliced	2 cloves garlic, sliced
2 green chillies, sliced lengthways	2 green chillies, sliced lengthwise
2 teaspoons red chilli powder	2 teaspoons red chilli powder
2 teaspoons garam masala	2 teaspoons garam masala
450g/1lb lean lamb, cut into small cubes	1lb lean lamb, cut into small cubes
1 tablespoon vinegar	1 tablespoon vinegar
salt to taste	salt to taste
2 tomatoes, quartered	2 tomatoes, quartered
1 tablespoon desiccated coconut	1 tablespoon shredded coconut

Heat the oil in a saucepan and fry the onion, garlic, chillies and chilli powder for about 2 minutes. Stir in the garam masala. Add the lamb, vinegar, salt and tomatoes and stir thoroughly. Cover and cook over a moderate heat for about 25 minutes until the meat is tender, stirring from time to time. Add a little water if necessary to prevent the meat from burning or sticking to the pan.

Sprinkle with the coconut and serve immediately.

Meat foogath

Gosht mazedaar

Foogath is strictly a southern Indian food phenomenon. It is the name given to a dish made from the left-overs of an already cooked meat or vegetable dish, usually by turning a curried dish into a dry one and vice versa. Mustard oil and coconut are nearly always included in this type of dish. Whereas the left-over curried ingredients can be given a new lease of life by being dressed in batter and fried into a snack, this particular recipe was initially a dry dish.

Preparation time 5 minutes   Cooking time 20–25 minutes   Serves 4

METRIC/IMPERIAL	AMERICAN
2 tablespoons mustard oil	3 tablespoons mustard oil
1 small onion, chopped	1 small onion, chopped
2 bay leaves	2 bay leaves
2 cloves	2 cloves
1 brown cardamom	1 brown cardamom
1 (2.5cm/1-inch) cinnamon stick	1 (1-inch) cinnamon stick
1 teaspoon garam masala	1 teaspoon garam masala
2 medium tomatoes, chopped	2 medium tomatoes, chopped
8 pieces of cooked dry meat	8 pieces of cooked dry meat
salt to taste	salt to taste
300ml/½ pint water	1¼ cups water
1 tablespoon desiccated coconut	1 tablespoon shredded coconut

Heat the oil in a saucepan and fry the onion, together with the bay leaves, cloves, cardamom and cinnamon, until golden. Stir in the garam masala and blend well. Add the tomatoes, meat and salt to taste. Cook over a moderate heat for about 5 minutes.

Pour in the water, lower the heat, cover and simmer gently for about 10–15 minutes until the water is reduced by half.

Sprinkle with the coconut and serve hot, to eat with a rice dish or bread.

Rabbit curry

Khargosh shorwedaar

•

This is another simple to make dish that you won't find in many Indian cookery books.

Preparation time 15 minutes   **Cooking time about 30 minutes**   **Serves 4**

METRIC/IMPERIAL	AMERICAN
1 medium rabbit, cut into small pieces	1 medium rabbit, cut into small pieces
salt as necessary	salt as necessary
100g/4oz ghee	½ cup ghee
1 large onion, minced	1 large onion, minced
2 cloves garlic, minced	2 cloves garlic, minced
1 (1cm/½-inch) piece fresh ginger root, minced	1 (½-inch) piece fresh ginger root, minced
2 bay leaves	2 bay leaves
1 brown cardamom	1 brown cardamom
2 (2.5cm/1-inch) cinnamon sticks	2 (1-inch) cinnamon sticks
½ teaspoon turmeric powder	½ teaspoon turmeric powder
1 tablespoon garam masala	1 tablespoon garam masala
½ teaspoon ground coriander	½ teaspoon ground coriander
1 tablespoon tomato purée	1 tablespoon tomato paste
2 tablespoons plain yoghurt	3 tablespoons plain yoghurt
300ml/½ pint milk	1¼ cups milk
salt to taste	salt to taste

Soak the rabbit pieces in salted water for about 10 minutes.

Heat the ghee in a saucepan and fry the onion, garlic and ginger over a moderate heat for about 1 minute. Add the bay leaves, cardamom and cinnamon and stir a few times. Add the turmeric, garam masala, coriander, tomato purée and yoghurt and stir for 2 minutes. Add the rabbit and simmer gently for another 5 minutes.

Pour in the milk and salt to taste, cover and simmer for about 20 minutes until the rabbit is tender, stirring occasionally. Serve hot, with a garnish or chutney of your choice.

Tandoori chicken

Tandoori murgha

•

*Most tandoori chicken recipes are time-consuming, but this one will not only save you
time, it will also please you with the result!*

Preparation time 15 minutes   **Cooking time about 30 minutes**   **Serves 4**

METRIC/IMPERIAL	AMERICAN
1 small oven-ready chicken	1 small roasting chicken
2 teaspoons salt, or to taste	2 teaspoons salt, or to taste
½ teaspoon ground black pepper	½ teaspoon ground black pepper
½ teaspoon red chilli powder	½ teaspoon red chilli powder
1 teaspoon cumin powder	1 teaspoon cumin powder
seeds of 2 green cardamoms, ground	seeds of 2 green cardamoms, ground
½ teaspoon garam masala	½ teaspoon garam masala
1 small onion, minced	1 small onion, minced
2 cloves garlic, minced	2 cloves garlic, minced
2 (142-ml/5-fl oz) cartons plain yoghurt, soured	1¼ cups plain yoghurt, soured
2 hard-boiled eggs	2 hard-cooked eggs
1 tablespoon desiccated coconut	1 tablespoon shredded coconut
1 tablespoon flaked almonds	1 tablespoon flaked almonds
1 teaspoon raisins	1 teaspoon raisins
1 teaspoon chironji nuts	1 teaspoon chironji nuts
225g/8oz melted butter	1 cup melted butter
½ teaspoon saffron, steeped in 1 tablespoon kewda water (see page 132)	½ teaspoon saffron, steeped in 1 tablespoon kewda water (see page 132)

Carefully prick the whole chicken with a fork. Then with a sharp knife, make several gashes over it, especially in the fleshy parts, making sure that the chicken stays intact. Place in a suitable cooking vessel and steam over simmering water for about 10 minutes.

Mix the salt, pepper, chilli and cumin powders, cardamom, garam masala, onion and garlic with the yoghurt and make a paste. Smear this paste thorough-ly all over the chicken inside and out. Place in a preheated moderate oven (160°C, 325°F, Gas Mark 3) and cook for about 10 minutes.

Remove from the oven and stuff the chicken cavity with the hard-boiled eggs, coconut, almonds, raisins and chironji nuts. Pour the butter all over the chicken and return to the oven for about 10 minutes until cooked. Sprinkle with the saffron mixture and serve hot.

Bombay duck with tomato

Battakh-machhli ki sabzi

●

Bombay duck is a herring-like fish, found in abundance around the western coast of India, near Bombay. Quite unlike fish, it likes to swim on the surface of the water, rather like a duck, and has thereby earned the nickname! It is cooked in many ways; here is one of them.

Preparation time 10 minutes   **Cooking time 20 minutes**   **Serves 4**

METRIC/IMPERIAL	AMERICAN
6 tablespoons ghee	7 tablespoons ghee
8 Bombay ducks, halved	8 Bombay ducks, halved
1 large onion, finely chopped	1 large onion, finely chopped
1 green chilli, chopped	1 green chilli, chopped
1 teaspoon ground coriander	1 teaspoon ground coriander
1 teaspoon turmeric powder	1 teaspoon turmeric powder
1 teaspoon red chilli powder	1 teaspoon red chilli powder
2 cloves garlic, crushed	2 cloves garlic, crushed
4 small potatoes, diced	4 small potatoes, diced
4 tomatoes, quartered	4 tomatoes, quartered
1 tablespoon desiccated coconut	1 tablespoon shredded coconut

Heat the ghee in a saucepan over a moderate heat and fry the Bombay ducks for 2 minutes. Drain on kitchen paper.

In the same ghee, fry the onion until golden. Stir in the chilli, coriander, turmeric, chilli powder and garlic, mix well. Add the potatoes, tomatoes and fried Bombay ducks, stir thoroughly. Cover, lower the heat and cook for 10 minutes.

Serve hot, sprinkled with coconut.

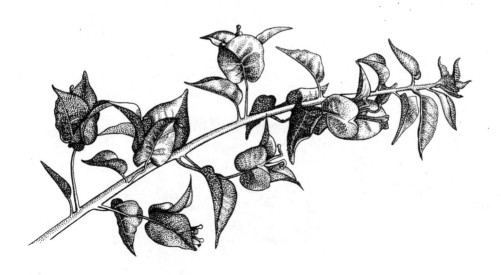

Fish in coconut milk

Doodhia machhli

●

Sole, plaice or any other white fish can be used in this particular recipe.

| Preparation time 10 minutes | Cooking time 25 minutes | Serves 4 |

METRIC/IMPERIAL	AMERICAN
2 cloves, ground	2 cloves, ground
4 green cardamoms, ground	4 green cardamoms, ground
2 green chillies, crushed	2 green chillies, crushed
2 cloves garlic, crushed	2 cloves garlic, crushed
1 (1cm/½-inch) piece fresh ginger root, crushed	1 (½-inch) piece fresh ginger root, crushed
1 tablespoon vindaloo powder	1 tablespoon vindaloo powder
salt to taste	salt to taste
lemon juice as necessary	lemon juice as necessary
450g/1lb fish fillets	1lb fish fillets
3 tablespoons mustard oil or ghee	¼ cup mustard oil or ghee
1 medium onion, thinly sliced	1 medium onion, thinly sliced
300ml/½ pint coconut milk	1¼ cups coconut milk
1 tablespoon chopped coriander leaves	1 tablespoon chopped coriander leaves

Mix the cloves, cardamoms, chillies, garlic, ginger, vindaloo powder and 1 teaspoon salt with sufficient lemon juice to make a paste. Smear the paste thickly over the fish fillets.

Heat the oil in a saucepan and fry the onion until golden. Add the fish pieces and fry until golden brown. Pour in the milk, together with salt to taste. Cover and cook over a moderate heat for about 15 minutes.

Serve hot, sprinkled with the coriander.

Baked mackerel

Dum machhli

| Preparation time 15 minutes | Cooking time about 20 minutes | Serves 4 |

METRIC/IMPERIAL	AMERICAN
salt to taste	salt to taste
1 teaspoon red chilli powder	1 teaspoon red chilli powder
¼ teaspoon green cardamom powder	¼ teaspoon green cardamom powder
pinch of garam masala	dash of garam masala
lemon juice as necessary	lemon juice as necessary
1 large mackerel (about 450g/1lb), cleaned	1 large mackerel (about 1lb), cleaned
ghee as necessary	ghee as necessary
½ teaspoon cumin powder	½ teaspoon cumin powder
½ teaspoon ground coriander	½ teaspoon ground coriander
½ teaspoon mango powder	½ teaspoon mango powder
1 green chilli, chopped	1 green chilli, chopped
½ tablespoon chopped coriander leaves	½ tablespoon chopped coriander leaves
1 medium potato, boiled, peeled and mashed	1 medium potato, boiled, peeled and mashed
1 tablespoon peas	1 tablespoon peas
1 tablespoon grated fresh coconut	1 tablespoon grated fresh coconut

Mix ½ teaspoon salt, half the chilli powder, all the cardamom powder and garam masala and enough lemon juice to make a thin paste. Brush this paste all over the fish, both inside and out.

Heat 1 tablespoon ghee in a frying pan and fry the cumin, coriander, mango powder, chilli, potato, peas and coconut, with the rest of the chilli powder and salt to taste, over a moderate heat for about 5 minutes. Remove from the heat and leave to cool a little.

Stuff this mixture inside the fish and place on a greased baking tray. Generously sprinkle ghee over the dish. Place in a preheated moderate oven (160°C, 325°F, Gas Mark 3) and bake for about 15 minutes until the fish is tender. Garnish as desired and serve whole. (For photograph see page 76.)

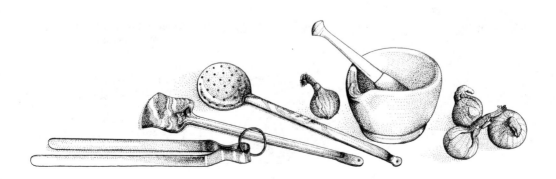

Mutton do-piazza

Gosht do-piazza

●

This is a dry dish with plenty of onion in it (see opposite). I have devised this recipe by combining the Punjabi and Kashmiri methods.

Preparation time 10 minutes   **Cooking time about 40 minutes**   **Serves 4**

METRIC/IMPERIAL	AMERICAN
100g/4oz ghee	½ cup ghee
450g/1lb onions, sliced	1lb onions, sliced
450g/1lb mutton, cut into pieces	1lb mutton, cut into pieces
600ml/1 pint plain yoghurt, beaten	2½ cups plain yoghurt, beaten
4 cloves	4 cloves
1 teaspoon red chilli powder	1 teaspoon red chilli powder
1 (2.5cm/1-inch) cinnamon stick	1 (1-inch) cinnamon stick
4 green cardamoms	4 green cardamoms
2 bay leaves	2 bay leaves
salt to taste	salt to taste
2 teaspoons poppy seeds, crushed	2 teaspoons poppy seeds, crushed
1 tablespoon flaked almonds	1 tablespoon flaked almonds
pinch of saffron strands	dash of saffron strands

Heat the ghee in a large saucepan and fry the onions. When they change colour, stir in the mutton, yoghurt, cloves, chilli powder, cinnamon, cardamoms and bay leaves. Bring to the boil and simmer for about 30 minutes until the meat is tender.

Add salt to taste, the poppy seeds and almonds and continue cooking until the mixture is completely dry. Scatter the saffron strands over the meat before serving.

Right Mutton dopiazza (see above) Sweet mango pickle (see page 110)

Overleaf Non-vegetarian meal 1: Parauntha (see page 31) 2: Green coriander chutney (see page 107) 3: Cucumber raita (see page 104) 4: Prawn soup (see page 23) 5: Chicken pullao (see page 74) 6: Pork vindaloo (see page 90) 7: Stuffed okra (see page 86) 8: Mango ice cream with vermicelli strands (see pages 118 and 120)

Chicken tango

Roghani murgha

●

This is a curry dish whose reddish colour (roghani) *comes from the tomato, chilli and turmeric and seems to 'dance' on the surface of the dish – hence my name for it!*

Preparation time 10 minutes	Cooking time about 35 minutes	Serves 4

METRIC/IMPERIAL	AMERICAN
100g/4oz ghee	½ cup ghee
1 medium onion, finely chopped	1 medium onion, finely chopped
2 bay leaves	2 bay leaves
4 cloves	4 cloves
1 (5cm/2-inch) cinnamon stick	1 (2-inch) cinnamon stick
1 brown cardamom	1 brown cardamom
4 black peppercorns	4 black peppercorns
1 teaspoon turmeric powder	1 teaspoon turmeric powder
1 teaspoon red chilli powder	1 teaspoon red chilli powder
1 tablespoon coriander seeds, dry roasted and ground	1 tablespoon coriander seeds, dry roasted and ground
4 cloves garlic, crushed	4 cloves garlic, crushed
1 (1cm/½-inch) piece fresh ginger root, crushed	1 (½-inch) piece fresh ginger root, crushed
1 small oven-ready chicken, cut into 8 pieces	1 small roasting chicken, cut into 8 pieces
4 tomatoes, quartered	4 tomatoes, quartered
2 teaspoons salt, or to taste	2 teaspoons salt, or to taste
300ml/½ pint warm water	1¼ cups warm water
½ teaspoon garam masala	½ teaspoon garam masala

Heat the ghee in a deep saucepan and fry the onion until golden. Add the bay leaves, cloves, cinnamon, cardamom and peppercorns and stir a few times. Stir in the turmeric, chilli, coriander, garlic and ginger. Blend together and fry for about 2 minutes. Add the chicken and tomatoes and cook, stirring, for 5 minutes.

Add the salt and water, cover tightly and simmer for about 20 minutes until the chicken is cooked. Lower the heat, sprinkle the garam masala over the chicken and cook for a further 5 minutes.

Serve hot with boiled rice, or one of the breads. (For photograph see opposite.)

Left Chicken tango (see above)
Mixed vegetable curry

Crab curry

Kekda rasedaar

Preparation time 10 minutes   Cooking time 15 minutes   Serves 6

METRIC/IMPERIAL	AMERICAN
2 tablespoons ghee	3 tablespoons ghee
1 medium onion, chopped	1 medium onion, chopped
4 cloves garlic, chopped	4 cloves garlic, chopped
½ teaspoon grated fresh ginger root	½ teaspoon grated fresh ginger root
2 green chillies, chopped	2 green chillies, chopped
1 teaspoon chopped curry leaves	1 teaspoon chopped curry leaves
6 crabs, boiled, shelled and flaked (1 per person)	6 crabs, boiled, shelled and flaked (1 per person)
salt to taste	salt to taste
150ml/¼ pint coconut milk	⅔ cup coconut milk
½ teaspoon red chilli powder	½ teaspoon red chilli powder
1 tablespoon desiccated coconut	1 tablespoon shredded coconut
1 tablespoon chopped coriander leaves	1 tablespoon chopped coriander leaves

Heat the ghee in a saucepan and fry the onion, garlic, ginger, chillies and curry leaves over a moderate heat for about 2 minutes. Add the flaked crab meat with salt to taste and fry for another 2–3 minutes. Pour in the milk and add the chilli powder, lower the heat and cook for about 10 minutes. Serve hot, sprinkled with the coconut and coriander leaves. (For photograph see page 76.)

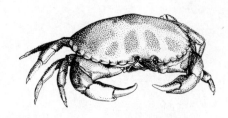

RAITAS, CHUTNEYS AND PICKLES
CHATPATI AUR MAZEDAAR

The dishes in this section liven up any meal, however insipid or bland. This they do by offering a sharp contrast of taste and flavour. Unlike their western counterparts, most of these preparations are quick and easy to make. Many of them will boost your appetite and are reputed to aid digestion.

These dishes go well with western foods too and are especially recommended for picnics and parties.

Raitas
Yoghurt plays a versatile role in the preparation of many Indian dishes, but it is of paramount importance in the raita dish. Raitas are yoghurt-based savoury preparations, usually made by combining yoghurt with a vegetable or fruit of your choice together with different seasonings. Raitas are always served as side dishes.

Some people, believing that the word 'raita' is derived from *rai* (mustard seeds), make a liberal use of mustard seeds in their raitas, others use chopped peanuts, almonds or cashews instead.

Chutneys
Most Indian meals are accompanied by a chutney or relish of some description. Chutneys can be made in a variety of ways, by mixing green fruits or vegetables with herbs, seasoning and other ingredients. They perk up the taste buds and stimulate the appetite. If the chutney of your choice proves too sour for you, add a little sugar or jaggery (see page 132) as desired.

Pickles
Indian pickles liven up any bland or plain food because of their pungency and flavour and also stimulate the appetite. Pickles are made from fresh fruits and vegetables. Their life-span varies from a few days to a few years, with many pickles (like wine) maturing with time.

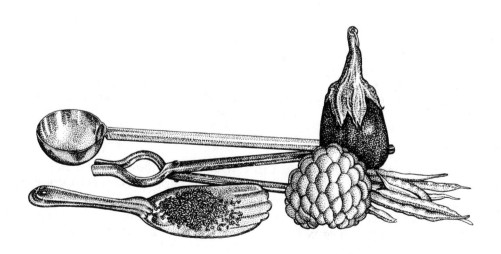

Cucumber raita

Kheere ka raita

Preparation time 10 minutes plus chilling time   Serves 6

METRIC/IMPERIAL	AMERICAN
2 (142ml/5fl oz) cartons plain yoghurt	1¼ cups plain yoghurt
salt to taste	salt to taste
½ teaspoon freshly ground black pepper	½ teaspoon freshly ground black pepper
225g/8oz cucumber, finely chopped	½lb cucumber, finely chopped
2 green chillies, finely chopped	2 green chillies, finely chopped
To garnish:	*To garnish:*
1 teaspoon white cumin seeds, dry roasted and ground	1 teaspoon white cumin seeds, dry roasted and ground
1 tablespoon chopped mint leaves	1 tablespoon chopped mint leaves

Beat the yoghurt with the salt and pepper to a smooth consistency. Add the cucumber and chillies and blend well. Garnish with cumin and mint. Serve chilled.

Batter-drop raita

Boondi ka raita

An exotic yoghurt-based mixture which can be eaten by itself, or as a side dish. Batter drops, boondi, *are available ready prepared.*

Preparation time 20 minutes plus chilling time   Serves 4

METRIC/IMPERIAL	AMERICAN
50g/2oz batter drops (*boondi*)	½ cup batter drops (*boondi*)
2 (142ml/5fl oz) cartons plain yoghurt	1¼ cups plain yoghurt
salt to taste	salt to taste
¼ teaspoon freshly ground black pepper	¼ teaspoon freshly ground black pepper
1 teaspoon red chilli powder	1 teaspoon red chilli powder
1 teaspoon white cumin seeds, dry roasted and ground	1 teaspoon white cumin seeds, dry roasted and ground
1 tablespoon chopped mint leaves	1 tablespoon chopped mint leaves

Soak the batter drops in warm water for about 10 minutes. Squeeze out the water by hand or place in a cloth, fold into a bundle and gently squeeze.

Place the yoghurt in a glass bowl and whisk to a smooth consistency. Stir in the salt and pepper and mix thoroughly. Add the batter drops, sprinkle with chilli powder, cumin and mint. Serve chilled. (For photograph see page 124.)

Spring onion raita

Hari pyaaz ka raita

•

This is a seasonal dish but it can also be made with ordinary onions.

Preparation time 15 minutes plus chilling time   Serves 4

METRIC/IMPERIAL	AMERICAN
2 (142ml/5fl oz) cartons plain yoghurt	1¼ cups plain yoghurt
salt to taste	salt to taste
½ teaspoon ground black pepper	½ teaspoon ground black pepper
4 small spring onions, chopped	4 small scallions, chopped
1 medium tomato, chopped	1 medium tomato, chopped
1 teaspoon mustard seeds, crushed	1 teaspoon mustard seeds, crushed
4 curry leaves, chopped	4 curry leaves, chopped
2 green chillies, chopped	2 green chillies, chopped
To garnish:	*To garnish:*
½ teaspoon white cumin seeds, dry roasted and ground	½ teaspoon white cumin seeds, dry roasted and ground
1 tablespoon chopped coriander leaves	1 tablespoon chopped coriander leaves

Beat the yoghurt with salt and pepper to a smooth consistency. Stir in the onions, tomato, mustard, curry leaves and chillies and blend thoroughly. Garnish with the cumin and coriander. Serve chilled. (For photograph see page 124.)

Cabbage raita

Karamkalle ka raita

Preparation time 15 minutes plus chilling time   Serves 4

METRIC/IMPERIAL	AMERICAN
600ml/1 pint plain yoghurt	2½ cups plain yoghurt
225g/8oz white cabbage, finely chopped	½lb white cabbage, finely chopped
2 green chillies, chopped	2 green chillies, chopped
1 teaspoon mustard seeds, coarsely ground	1 teaspoon mustard seeds, coarsely ground
salt to taste	salt to taste
1 teaspoon white cumin seeds, dry roasted and ground	1 teaspoon white cumin seeds, dry roasted and ground
1 tablespoon finely chopped coriander leaves	1 tablespoon finely chopped coriander leaves

Whisk yoghurt to a smooth consistency. Add the cabbage, chillies, mustard, salt, cumin and mix thoroughly. Sprinkle with chopped coriander. Serve chilled.

Cumin seeds refresher

Zeera jal

Although usually served with the chaat dish, flour wafers, golgappa (see page 61), it can be served by itself, too. Tamarind pulp is available in tins or bottles at Indian grocers.

Preparation time 25 minutes plus chilling time   Serves 4

METRIC/IMPERIAL	AMERICAN
50g/2oz tamarind pulp	2oz tamarind pulp
600ml/1 pint warm water	2½ cups warm water
½ teaspoon garam masala	½ teaspoon garam masala
pinch of asafoetida powder	dash of asafoetida powder
salt to taste	salt to taste
½ teaspoon black salt	½ teaspoon black salt
1 teaspoon white cumin seeds, dry roasted and ground	1 teaspoon white cumin seeds, dry roasted and ground
½ teaspoon red chilli powder	½ teaspoon red chilli powder
1½ teaspoons lemon juice	1½ teaspoons lemon juice
1 teaspoon sugar	1 teaspoon sugar
1 tablespoon chopped mint leaves	1 tablespoon chopped mint leaves

Soak the tamarind pulp in the warm water for about 15 minutes. Then mash and blend it thoroughly. Push the liquid through a sieve and throw away the residue. Add the garam masala, asafoetida powder, salts, cumin, chilli powder, lemon juice, sugar and mint. Mix together thoroughly.

Serve chilled and stir before use. (For photograph see page 44.)

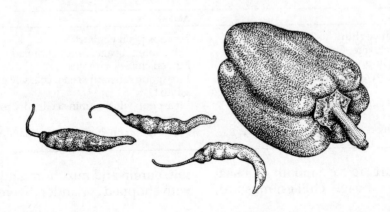

Green coriander chutney

Hari dhania ki chatni

A delicious chutney which can also be prepared with mint leaves. Add a little sugar, if it proves too sour. This chutney should be made fresh every time.

Preparation time 10 minutes plus chilling time   Serves 4

METRIC/IMPERIAL	AMERICAN
4 tablespoons coriander leaves	5 tablespoons coriander leaves
1 green chilli, quartered	1 green chilli, quartered
salt to taste	salt to taste
juice of 4 juicy lemons	juice of 4 juicy lemons

Coarsely grind the coriander, chilli and salt together. Add the lemon juice and mix thoroughly. Serve chilled. (For photograph see page 100.)

Saambhar sauce

Saambhar

This dish is a popular accompaniment to most south Indian dishes. You can use seasonal vegetables of your choice, eg. cauliflower, aubergine, potato, carrots or whole green chillies.

Preparation time 10 minutes   Cooking time about 25 minutes   Serves 4

METRIC/IMPERIAL	AMERICAN
2 tablespoons saambhar powder (see page 16)	2 tablespoons saambhar powder (see page 16)
600ml/1 pint water	2½ cups water
salt to taste	salt to taste
1 teaspoon tamarind chutney (see page 109)	1 teaspoon tamarind chutney (see page 109)
100g/4oz mixed fresh vegetables, cut into large pieces	¼lb mixed fresh vegetables, cut into large pieces
1 tablespoon chopped coriander leaves	1 tablespoon chopped coriander leaves

Place the saambhar powder and water into a large saucepan and bring to the boil over a high heat. Lower the heat, stir in the salt and tamarind chutney and cook for 5–7 minutes. Add the vegetables and cook for a further 10 minutes or so until they are tender and the liquid is the required consistency.

Serve steaming hot, sprinkled with the coriander.

Garlic chutney

Lahsun ki chatni

METRIC/IMPERIAL	AMERICAN
4 cloves garlic, thickly sliced	4 cloves garlic, thickly sliced
2 fresh green chillies, halved	2 fresh green chillies, halved
1½ teaspoons white cumin seeds	1½ teaspoons white cumin seeds
1 tablespoon coriander leaves	1 tablespoon coriander leaves
salt to taste	salt to taste
4 tablespoons lemon juice	⅓ cup lemon juice
grated onion, to garnish	grated onion, to garnish

Coarsely grind the garlic, chillies, cumin, coriander and salt together by hand or in an electric grinder. Add the lemon juice and stir a few times. Garnish with the grated onion. (For photograph see page 76.)

Coconut chutney

Naariyal ki chatni
•

This chutney is normally served with south Indian dishes.

Preparation time 10 minutes plus chilling time   Cooking time 5 minutes   Serves 6

METRIC/IMPERIAL	AMERICAN
300ml/½ pint plain yoghurt	1¼ cups plain yoghurt
2 tablespoons grated fresh coconut	3 tablespoon grated fresh coconut
2 tablespoons mixed black bean and pigeon peas powders *(urad* and *toor dall)*	2 tablespoons mixed black bean and pigeon peas powders *(urad* and *toor dall)*
½ teaspoon grated fresh ginger root	½ teaspoon grated fresh ginger root
2 green chillies, crushed	2 green chillies, crushed
salt to taste	salt to taste
1 tablespoon melted ghee	1 tablespoon melted ghee
1 teaspoon mustard seeds	1 teaspoon mustard seeds
1 tablespoon chopped coriander leaves	1 tablespoon chopped coriander leaves

Beat the yoghurt and stir in the coconut. Add the dall powders, ginger, chillies and salt and whisk thoroughly.

Heat the ghee in a saucepan and add the mustard. Stir a couple of times and then stir in yoghurt mixture. Cook for 2 minutes over medium heat. Remove the pan from the heat, add the coriander and transfer the contents to a serving dish. Serve chilled. (For photograph see page 124.)

Tamarind chutney

Khatmitthi raani

Preparation time 25 minutes plus chilling time   Serves 4

METRIC/IMPERIAL	AMERICAN
25g/1oz tamarind pulp (see page 133)	1oz tamarind pulp (see page 133)
150ml/¼ pint warm water	⅔ cup warm water
salt to taste	salt to taste
25g/1oz jaggery (see page 132) or sugar	1oz jaggery (see page 132) or sugar
1 teaspoon red chilli powder	1 teaspoon red chilli powder

Soak the tamarind in the warm water for about 15 minutes and mash it into the water; blend thoroughly. Push the liquid through a clean cloth, and throw away the residue. Stir in the salt, sugar and chilli powder and mix well. Serve chilled.

Chilli fried pickle

Mirch ka bhuna achaar

Preparation time 15 minutes   Cooking time 5 minutes   Serves 4

METRIC/IMPERIAL	AMERICAN
1 tablespoon coriander seeds	1 tablespoon coriander seeds
½ teaspoon white cumin seeds	½ teaspoon white cumin seeds
½ teaspoon fenugreek seeds	½ teaspoon fenugreek seeds
½ teaspoon nigella (see page 132)	½ teaspoon nigella (see page 132)
1 tablespoon fennel seeds	1 tablespoon fennel seeds
pinch of asafoetida powder	dash of asafoetida powder
1 teaspoon salt	1 teaspoon salt
1 teaspoon mango powder	1 teaspoon mango powder
2 tablespoons oil	3 tablespoons oil
8 large red chillies, slit lengthways	8 large red chillies, slit lengthwise

Heat a griddle or heavy frying pan over a moderate heat and roast the coriander, cumin and fenugreek seeds, nigella and fennel until they give off an aromatic smell. Grind by hand or in an electric grinder. Stir in the asafoetida, salt, mango powder and half the oil and blend thoroughly to make a stuffing. Divide the stuffing into 8 portions. Fill each chilli with a portion of stuffing.

Heat the remaining oil in a shallow frying pan with a lid. Add the stuffed chillies, cover tightly and cook over a moderate heat for about 2 minutes. Turn the chillies over, cover again and cook for another 2–3 minutes. Serve hot or cold.

Sweet mango pickle

Aam ka meetha achaar

Preparation time 15 minutes   Cooking time 35 minutes   Serves 15

METRIC/IMPERIAL	AMERICAN
900g/2lb jaggery (see page 132)	2lb jaggery (see page 132)
1.15 litres/2 pints water	5 cups water
1kg/2lb green mangoes, grated	2lb green mangoes, grated
2 teaspoons salt	2 teaspoons salt
1 teaspoon red chilli powder	1 teaspoon red chilli powder
15g/½oz nigella (see page 132)	½oz nigella (see page 132)
6g/¼oz fenugreek seeds, dry roasted and ground	¼oz fenugreek seeds, dry roasted and ground
25g/1oz coriander seeds, dry roasted and ground	1oz coriander seeds, dry roasted and ground

Place the jaggery and water in a deep saucepan and bring to the boil. Add the mango and cook over a moderate heat for about 15 minutes until the water evaporates and the mixture thickens. Stir in the salt, chilli powder, nigella, fenugreek and coriander seeds. Continue cooking for another 10 minutes until all are well blended. Leave to cool.

Store in a lidded jar and serve when required. Replace the lid after each use. (For photograph see page 100.)

Lemon sour pickle

Chatpate neebu

Preparation time 10 minutes plus maturing time   Serves about 30

METRIC/IMPERIAL	AMERICAN
½ teaspoon asafoetida powder	½ teaspoon asafoetida powder
8 juicy lemons, quartered	8 juicy lemons, quartered
4 tablespoons salt	5 tablespoons salt
1 teaspoon carom seeds	1 teaspoon carom seeds
juice of 4 lemons	juice of 4 lemons

Take a clean, dry, glass jar with a lid and sprinkle the asafoetida powder in the base. Drop in the lemon pieces and then stir in the salt. Add the carom seeds and pour in the lemon juice. Cover tightly and place in the sun or warmest place in the house for about 1 week until the lemon skin is soft. Shake the jar at least once a day, and shake before use. (For photograph see page 124.)

SWEETS, ICE CREAM AND PRESERVES

MITHAIYAAN, KULFI AUR MURABBE

Indian sweets symbolise fun and festivity and are an institution in themselves. Being the third largest sugar producers in the world, it is hardly surprising that the people of India have an incomparable sweet tooth! Almost every day in India is a day of celebration for something. Literally hundreds of festivals are observed there, and for every festival there is a particular sweet to be made. Besides, 'sweetening the mouth' of one's friends and relatives to mark a happy occasion or event is obligatory for every host. Furthermore, Indians offer sweets to please the children and placate the gods. Sweets are also offered as a token of love, friendship and hospitality.

Most Indian sweets are milk-based and are therefore nourishing as well as tasty.

Many of these dishes are quite simple to make, although the methods of using milk for these preparations may not be common knowledge here in the West, nevertheless, many Indian sweets are very popular in the West. Do adjust the quantity of sugar according to your liking.

In order to make sweet dishes look more attractive, Indians decorate their sweets with edible gold and silver foils, which are very delicate and should be handled with great care. These edible foils are supposed to have digestive qualities as well!

A small quantity of coarsely ground green cardamom seeds sprinkled over the top of the puddings is another way of adding a decorative touch.

Coconut balls

Gari ke laddu

Preparation time 15 minutes	Cooking time 15 minutes	Serves 4

METRIC/IMPERIAL	AMERICAN
225g/8oz dried milk (*khoya*, see page 19)	½lb dried milk (*khoya*, see page 19)
175g/6oz sugar	¾ cup sugar
175g/6oz desiccated coconut	2 cups shredded coconut

Place the dried milk in a saucepan over a low heat. Stir in half each of the sugar and coconut. When the dried milk turns golden, after about 10 minutes, remove the mixture from the heat. Add the rest of the sugar and mix well.

Place the remaining coconut in a small bowl. Make small walnut size balls from the milk mixture. Roll them in the coconut to coat, and serve.

Ambrosial delectation

Madhur sambhog

Preparation time 20 minutes	Cooking time 30 minutes	Serves 4

METRIC/IMPERIAL	AMERICAN
225g/8oz plain flour	2 cups all-purpose flour
450g/1lb ghee	2 cups ghee
25g/1oz semolina	1oz semolina
100g/4oz dried milk (*khoya*, see page 19)	¼lb dried milk (*khoya*, see page 19)
50g/2oz mixed nuts (chironji, flaked almonds, pistachios and desiccated coconut), chopped	½ cup mixed nuts (chironji, flaked almonds, pistachios and shredded coconut), chopped
25g/1oz sugar candy, *misree*, coarsely ground	1oz sugar candy, *misree*, coarsely ground
pinch of green cardamom powder	dash of green cardamom powder
8 cloves	8 cloves
600ml/1 pint 2-string sugar syrup (see page 19)	2½ cups, 2-string sugar syrup (see page 19)
rose water, to serve	rose water, to serve
edible silver foils, to decorate	edible silver foils, to decorate

Place the flour in a bowl and rub in 100g/4oz/½ cup of the ghee. Add sufficient water to knead into a medium pliable dough. Divide into 8 portions. Flatten each portion and roll it out into a 2.5cm/1-inch round. Cover with a damp cloth.

Heat 1 tablespoon of the ghee in a saucepan and fry the semolina for about 2 minutes until golden. Add the dried milk, chopped nuts, sugar candy and cardamom and blend thoroughly. Divide this mixture into 8 portions.

Take one dough round, heap one portion of the semolina mixture in the middle and fold the dough over the mixture into a square package – back to front and then side to side. Secure its shape by inserting a clove in the middle. Make the other squares in the same way.

Heat the remaining ghee in a *kadhai* or deep fryer and fry all the 'packages' over a low heat for about 10 minutes until they are light golden in colour all over. Remove and drain on absorbent kitchen paper.

Reheat the syrup and add the packages to it. After about 10 minutes, when they are fully soaked and puff up, drain them and place on a serving dish. Sprinkle with the rose water, cover with the foils and serve.

Banana roundels

Kele ke meethe bade

Preparation time 10 minutes　　**Cooking time 10 minutes**　　**Serves 6**

METRIC/IMPERIAL	AMERICAN
2 large ripe bananas	2 large ripe bananas
100g/4oz rice flour	1 cup rice flour
2 tablespoons castor sugar	3 tablespoons sugar
pinch of salt	dash of salt
coconut milk as necessary	coconut milk as necessary
ghee for deep frying	ghee for deep frying

Peel and cut the bananas into fairly thin slices and pat dry. Beat the flour, half the sugar and the salt with the coconut milk to make a thick batter. Heat the ghee in a *kadhai* or a deep fryer. Dip each banana slice into the batter and fry, several at a time, until golden. Remove and drain on absorbent kitchen paper. Sprinkle with the remaining sugar. Serve hot. (For photograph see page 76.)

Almond toffee

Baadaam burfi

Preparation time 15 minutes　　**Cooking time 20 minutes**　　**Serves 6**

METRIC/IMPERIAL	AMERICAN
450g/1lb ground almonds	4 cups ground almonds
ghee as necessary	ghee as necessary
225g/8oz dried milk (*khoya*, see page 19)	½lb dried milk (*khoya*, see page 19)
1-string sugar syrup (see page 19), to taste	1-string sugar syrup (see page 19), to taste
1 tablespoon green cardamom powder	1 tablespoon green cardamom powder

Mix the ground almonds with sufficient water to make a thick paste. Heat 50g/2oz/ ¼ cup ghee in a pan and fry the paste until golden (about 15 minutes). Add the dried milk and mix thoroughly. Add 1 tablespoon ghee, pour in about 150ml/¼ pint/⅔ cup sugar syrup and blend well.

Grease the base of a large platter with ghee and sprinkle the cardamom powder on it. Spread the almond mixture evenly on the platter and leave to cool.

With a knife, cut the setting mixture into desired shapes, turn them over and serve, decorated with edible gold foils if you wish. (For photograph see page 124.)

Rice pudding
Chaawal ki kheer

●

This is the most popular Indian pudding known in the West, but it is so different and much tastier than the English variety!

Preparation time 10 minutes   **Cooking time 45 minutes**   **Serves 4**

METRIC/IMPERIAL	AMERICAN
1 teaspoon ghee	1 teaspoon ghee
4 tablespoons Basmati rice, washed	5 tablespoons Basmati rice, washed
2 tablespoons sugar	3 tablespoons sugar
1 litre/1¾ pints creamy milk	4¼ cups creamy milk
1 tablespoon sultanas, pre-soaked	1 tablespoon golden raisins, pre-soaked
1 teaspoon flaked pistachios	1 teaspoon flaked pistachios
1 tablespoon flaked almonds	1 tablespoon flaked almonds
½ teaspoon green cardamom powder	½ teaspoon green cardamom powder
4 edible silver foils, to decorate	4 edible silver foils, to decorate

Heat the ghee in a saucepan and fry the rice over a low heat for about 5 minutes. Add the sugar and milk and stir well. Simmer for about 25 minutes, stirring from time to time, until the milk is reduced by half. Add the sultanas and nuts and simmer for another 15 minutes.

Serve hot or cold, sprinkled with the cardamom powder and decorated with silver foils. (For photograph see page 124.)

Note: You can make makhana (roasted lotus seeds) pudding in the same way; just substitute 25g/1oz makhanas (see page 132) for rice.

Sweet yoghurt in saffron

Shrikhand

A delicious offering from the Maharashtra region of India. Eat it by itself or with any of the Indian breads.

Preparation time 10 minutes plus dripping and chilling time   Serves 4

METRIC/IMPERIAL	AMERICAN
4 (142ml/5fl oz) cartons plain yoghurt	2½ cups plain yoghurt
175g/6oz sugar	¾ cup sugar
1 teaspoon green cardamom seeds, crushed	1 teaspoon green cardamom seeds, crushed
1 teaspoon grated pistachios	1 teaspoon grated pistachios
1 teaspoon chopped chironji nuts	1 teaspoon chopped chironji nuts
1 teaspoon flaked almonds	1 teaspoon flaked almonds
pinch of grated nutmeg	dash of grated nutmeg
1 teaspoon rose water	1 teaspoon rose water
pinch of saffron, crushed	dash of saffron, crushed
fresh rose petals, to decorate	fresh rose petals, to decorate

Place the yoghurt in a clean muslin cloth, fold it up into a loose bundle and hang for about 2 hours until the excess moisture has dripped through. Transfer the yoghurt in the muslin to a bowl, add the sugar and whisk until the mixture is smooth. Stir in the cardamom, nuts, nutmeg and rose water and blend thoroughly. Sprinkle with the saffron. Serve chilled, decorated with rose petals.

Carrot halwa

Gaajar ka halwa

Halwas are a sweet dish, usually served in India at breakfast time. In some regions of India, halwas are served with afternoon tea as well. Most of them are served hot, but they can be eaten cold, too. Some, like the carrot halwa, can be reheated and served a second or third time without losing their quality or taste.

Preparation time about 10 minutes   Cooking time 35 minutes   Serves 6

METRIC/IMPERIAL	AMERICAN
450g/1lb carrots, grated	1lb carrots, grated
300ml/½ pint milk	1¼ cups milk
225g/8oz ghee	1 cup ghee
100g/4oz dried milk (*khoya*, see page 19)	¼lb dried milk (*khoya*, see page 19)
100g/4oz sugar	½ cup sugar
100g/4oz mixed dried fruit and nuts (chopped sultanas, almonds and pistachios)	1 cup mixed dried fruit and nuts (chopped golden raisins, almonds and pistachios)
½ teaspoon coarsely ground green cardamom powder	½ teaspoon coarsely ground green cardamom powder
edible gold foils, to serve	edible gold foils, to serve

Place the carrots and milk in a saucepan and bring to the boil. Lower the heat and cook for about 20 minutes until the milk is fully absorbed into the carrots, stirring occasionally.

Heat the ghee in a *kadhai* or frying pan and fry the dried milk until golden. Add the sugar and carrot and stir thoroughly until the mixture begins to release the ghee. Stir in the dried fruit and nuts together with the cardamom powder and blend well. Remove from the heat and serve hot. Decorate each serving with an edible gold foil.

Note: Any left-overs can be stored in the refrigerator and reheated before use.

Dall sweet in syrup

Imarti

•

This delectable dish should be eaten hot when crisp and fresh.

Preparation time 15 minutes plus soaking time   **Cooking time 15 minutes**   **Serves 6**

METRIC/IMPERIAL	AMERICAN
225g/8oz skinless black beans *(urad dall)*	1 cup skinless black beans *(urad dall)*
½ teaspoon bicarbonate of soda	½ teaspoon baking soda
900g/2lb sugar	4 cups sugar
½ teaspoon green cardamom powder	½ teaspoon green cardamom powder
4 drops kewda essence (see page 132)	4 drops kewda essence (see page 132)
ghee for frying	ghee for frying

Soak the dall in water for about 2 hours. Drain out the water, stir in the baking powder and grind finely by hand or with an electric grinder into a thick batter.

Make a 1-string syrup with the sugar (see page 19) and add to it the cardamom powder and kewda essence.

Take a clean thick cloth, about 23-cm/9-inch square and make a hole in the middle. Dampen this cloth with water and put about an eighth of the batter on it. Fold all the four corners together into a bundle and hold tight.

Heat sufficient ghee for shallow frying in a frying pan over a moderate heat. Squeeze the bundle of batter over the frying pan and make a panful of small flower shapes of batter. Let them sizzle for a minute or so; turn over and cook in the same way on the other side. When they are deep golden, remove and immerse them in the syrup for about 5 minutes until it is fully soaked into their pipes. Remove from the syrup, drain and serve hot.

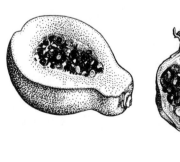
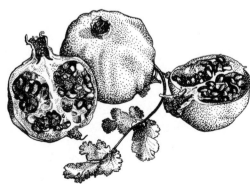

Indian ice cream
Kulfi

Indian ice cream is yet to be discovered by the West! It is rich in content, scrumptious in taste and becomes even more tasty when served with *faaluda* – a delicious vermicelli-like dish. Besides, Indian ice cream is so easy to make that it is bound to be popular with the young and old alike

Traditionally, it is made in conical metal moulds (see page 12 for a picture of these moulds), which after being filled are immersed into a large earthen pitcher, full of ice and a mixture of salt and saltpetre, for freezing. You may however use plastic ice-cube trays, or any other suitable container, and freeze your ice cream in a freezer. Indian ice cream is harder than ordinary Western ice cream and often has ice crystals in it, a little like sorbet, but it melts rather faster as no setting agent is added to it normally. Therefore, you should transfer the ice cream from the freezer to the refrigerator when it is firm and serve straight from there.

Mango ice cream
Aam ki kulfi
●

This is the Indian kulfi par excellence!

Preparation time 10 minutes plus freezing time   Cooking time 20 minutes   Serves 6

METRIC/IMPERIAL	AMERICAN
900ml/1½ pints creamy milk	3¾ cups creamy milk
2 tablespoons sugar	3 tablespoons sugar
flesh of 2 ripe mangoes	flesh of 2 ripe mangoes
6 green cardamoms' seeds, coarsely ground	6 green cardamoms' seeds, coarsely ground
4 blanched almonds, finely chopped	4 blanched almonds, finely chopped
rose water, to serve	rose water, to serve
vermicelli strands (*faaluda*), to serve (optional, see page 120)	vermicelli strands (*faaluda*), to serve (optional, see page 120)

Boil the milk and sugar together, stirring constantly, and go on cooking until the milk is reduced to just over half. Remove from the heat, add the sugar, mango flesh and ground cardamom seeds and blend thoroughly, either by hand or with an electric grinder. When the mixture is cool, pour it into the containers and freeze for a minimum of 1 hour. Serve with a sprinkling of rose water and vermicelli strands (*faaluda*) if desired. (For photograph see page 100.)

Pistachio ice cream
Pishte ki kulfi

Preparation time 10 minutes plus freezing time **Cooking time about 10 minutes**
Serves 6

METRIC/IMPERIAL	AMERICAN
225g/8oz pistachios	½lb pistachios
150ml/¼ pint milk	⅔ cup milk
2 (114ml/4-fl oz cartons single cream	1 cup light cream
2 tablespoons sugar	3 tablespoons sugar
pinch of salt	dash of salt
rose water, to serve	rose water, to serve

Grind the pistachios in a little of the milk by hand, gradually adding the rest of the milk. Mix well. Add the cream, sugar and salt and mix thoroughly. Place the mixture in a saucepan and cook over a moderate heat for 10 minutes, stirring constantly. Remove the pan from the heat and leave to cool. Pour the cooled mixture into the containers and freeze for a minimum of 1 hour. Serve straight from the refrigerator, and sprinkle with rose water. (For photograph see page 124.)

Cold vermicelli strands

Faaluda

●

This is often served with Indian ice cream; 1 tablespoon is usually sufficient for each serving. It can also be eaten by itself sprinkled with a little sugar syrup, rose water and some crushed ice.

Preparation time about 5 minutes	Cooking time about 20 minutes	Serves 6

METRIC/IMPERIAL	AMERICAN
225g/8oz cornflour	2 cups cornstarch
900ml/1½ pints water	3¾ cups water

Make a paste with the cornflour and a little of the water, making sure there are no lumps. Then stir in the rest of the water and transfer the contents to a saucepan. Place the pan over a moderate heat and bring to the boil, stirring continuously. Cook over a low heat until the mixture thickens and becomes translucent.

Stand a perforated spoon or *jhanna* (see page 11) over a large deep saucepan, full of cold water. Push the mixture over the perforations and large vermicelli strands will fall into the water.

Leave in clear cold water and serve straight from the water, strained. (For photograph see page 100.)

Pineapple ice lolly

Anannas ki baraf chuski

Preparation time 10 minutes plus freezing time	Serves 6

METRIC/IMPERIAL	AMERICAN
2 egg yolks	2 egg yolks
150ml/¼ pint sugar syrup (see page 19)	⅔ cup sugar syrup (see page 19)
300ml/½ pint fresh pineapple juice	1¼ cups fresh pineapple juice
½ teaspoon lemon juice	½ teaspoon lemon juice
150ml/¼ pint water	⅔ cup water
rose water, to serve	rose water, to serve

Whisk the egg yolks into the sugar syrup. Add the fruit juices and water and mix thoroughly. Fill this liquid into ice lolly moulds or suitable freezer containers, pushing a stick into each, and freeze. Serve sprinkled with rose water.

Preserves
Murabbe

Preserves are a popular form of confection in India. Unlike ordinary sweetmeats, they last a long time and come in handy when that unexpected guest arrives! Wholesome and sustaining, preserves are generally made from fruits or vegetables. The preparation of Indian preserves involves the cleaning of the fruit, pricking with a fork to increase its soaking capacity, boiling in water and then immersing in sugar syrup (see page 19). The sugar syrup required for these preserves is usually of 2-string consistency. Preserves are normally served decorated with edible silver or gold foils to match the colour of the dish. They should be stored in dry, sterilized and airtight jars until required.

Pear preserve
Naashpaati ka murabba

Preparation time 10 minutes   Cooking time 25 minutes   Serves 4

METRIC/IMPERIAL	AMERICAN
4 small firm pears	4 small firm pears
300ml/½ pint 1-string sugar syrup (see page 19)	1¼ cups 1-string sugar syrup (see page 19)
2 tablespoons rose water	3 tablespoons rose water
pinch of saffron, crushed	dash of saffron, crushed
edible gold foils, to decorate	edible gold foils, to decorate

Peel the pears and cut off their tops and bottoms. Prick them all over with a fork. Place in a saucepan with enough water to cover them. Place over a moderate heat and bring to the boil a couple of times. Remove and drain off the water.

Pour the sugar syrup in a saucepan, add the pears and simmer over a low heat until the pears are cooked and the syrup is thickened. Remove from the heat and leave to cool. Steep the saffron in the rose water and sprinkle over the pears. Store in a sterilized and airtight container. Serve hot or cold, decorated with the foils.

Lemon preserve

Neebu ka murabba

Preparation time 10 minutes   **Cooking time 25 minutes**   **Serves 4**

METRIC/IMPERIAL	AMERICAN
8 juicy lemons	8 juicy lemons
1 teaspoon edible lime powder	1 teaspoon edible lime powder
300ml/½ pint sugar syrup (see page 19)	1¼ cups sugar syrup (see page 19)
edible silver or gold foils, to decorate	edible silver or gold foils, to decorate

Peel the lemons and prick them all over with a fork. Place in a deep saucepan with enough water to cover them. Add the lime and bring to the boil a couple of times. Remove from the heat and drain off the water. Wash the lemons several times with clean water.

Pour the sugar syrup in a saucepan, add the lemons, cover and simmer over a low heat until the lemons are cooked and the syrup is thickened. Remove from the heat and leave to cool. Store in a sterilized and airtight container. Serve decorated with suitable foils.

COLD SOFT DRINKS
RIMJHIM PHUHAAR

After a sweltering summer day, freshly made cold soft drinks go down very well! Indian hosts often choose to offer their guests drinks freshly made from fruits, grown in abundance in their country, together with other exotic oriental ingredients. These drinks are not complicated to make, in fact most of them are incredibly quick and easy. Besides, when you make them yourself, the drinks do not cost the earth and you are sure of their quality.

Pomegranate shower
Anaar bauchhaar
●

This drink is very refreshing and restores composure after a hard day's work.

Preparation time 10 minutes plus chilling time   Serves 6

METRIC/IMPERIAL	AMERICAN
4 tablespoons sugar	5 tablespoons sugar
600ml/1 pint water	2½ cups water
300ml/½ pint fresh pomegranate juice	1¼ cups fresh pomegranate juice
6 drops red food colouring	6 drops red food coloring
1 tablespoon rose water	1 tablespoon rose water
lemon slices, to decorate	lemon slices, to decorate

Whisk the sugar and water together until the sugar is completely dissolved. Stir in the pomegranate juice, food colouring and rose water and mix thoroughly. Serve chilled, decorated with lemon slices.

Note: Pomegranate juice may be purchased but you can also crush the seeds of the fruit to squeeze out the juice.

Lemon sharbat

Mohit sheetal

•

*One of the most popular drinks, particularly with athletes as it is especially refreshing
after strenuous activity. Amounts of lemon juice and sugar may be adjusted
according to personal taste.*

Preparation time 5 minutes   Serves 6

METRIC/IMPERIAL	AMERICAN
900ml/1½ pints water	3¾ cups water
1½ tablespoons lemon juice	2 tablespoons lemon juice
3 tablespoons sugar	4 tablespoons sugar
1 teaspoon rose water	1 teaspoon rose water
12 ice cubes, crushed	12 ice cubes, crushed
lemon slices, to decorate	lemon slices, to decorate

Mix all the ingredients, reserving half the ice, and whisk briskly. Serve topped with crushed ice and decorated with lemon slices. (For photograph see opposite.)

Left Hukkah (see page 129)

Right Sweets and drinks (from the top)
Lemon sharbat (see above) Watermelon punch
(see page 126) Rice pudding (see page 114)
Almond toffee (see page 113) Pistachio ice cream
(see page 119)

Overleaf Raitas and chutneys (from the top
clockwise) Batter-drop raita (see page 104) Sweet
mango pickle (see page 110) Coconut chutney (see
page 108) Lemon sour pickle (see page 110) Spring
onion raita (see page 105) Garlic chutney (see page
108)

Mango frappé

Peeyush aam panna

This exquisite drink is sweet and sour.

Preparation time 10 minutes plus chilling time   **Cooking time 10 minutes**   **Serves 6**

METRIC/IMPERIAL	AMERICAN
6 medium green mangoes	6 medium green mangoes
900ml/1½ pints water	3¾ cups water
1 teaspoon salt	1 teaspoon salt
½ teaspoon pounded dried red chillies or red chilli powder	½ teaspoon pounded dried red chillies or red chilli powder
1 teaspoon white cumin seeds, dry roasted and ground	1 teaspoon white cumin seeds, dry roasted and ground
2 tablespoons sugar	3 tablespoons sugar
2 tablespoons chopped mint leaves	3 tablespoons chopped mint leaves
12 ice cubes, crushed	12 ice cubes, crushed

Place the mangoes with water to cover in a saucepan and bring to the boil. Simmer for 10 minutes. Drain off the water and then peel, stone and pulp the mango flesh with a spoon.

Place the pulp in a deep bowl. Add the water, salt, chillies, cumin and sugar and whisk thoroughly. Stir in the mint and whisk again. Transfer the contents to a jug. Serve chilled, with crushed ice.

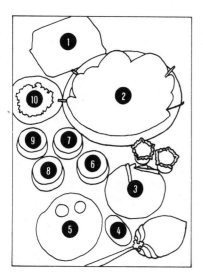

Left The conclusion to a meal – the paan ritual
1: Paandaan 2: Paan 3: Beedis 4: Lime paste 5: Betel nuts 6: Desiccated coconut 7: Pistachio nuts 8: Green cardamom 9: Aniseed 10: Sugar candy

Rain of nectar

Madhu varsha

•

This drink is also known as panchaamrit *and is often served on special occasions.*
Make fresh each time.

Preparation time 5 minutes   Serves 6

METRIC/IMPERIAL	AMERICAN
600ml/1 pint milk	2½ cups milk
2 (142ml/5-fl oz) cartons plain yoghurt	1¼ cups plain yoghurt
2 tablespoons sugar	3 tablespoons sugar
25g/1oz honey	2 tablespoons honey
225g/8oz mixed chopped dried fruit and nuts (sultanas, makhanas, coconut, chironji)	2 cups mixed chopped dried fruit and nuts (golden raisins, makhanas, coconut, chironji)

Whisk the milk and yoghurt together. Stir in the sugar and mix until dissolved. Add the honey and then the chopped dried fruit and nuts and mix thoroughly. Serve in small glasses. (For photograph see page 77.)

Water melon punch

Manoj tarbooz tarang

Preparation time 10 minutes   Serves 6

METRIC/IMPERIAL	AMERICAN
225g/8oz ripe seedless water melon flesh	½lb ripe seedless water melon flesh
4 tablespoons sugar	5 tablespoons sugar
600ml/1 pint water	2½ cups water
seeds of 4 green cardamoms, ground	seeds of 4 green cardamoms, ground
12 ice cubes, crushed	12 ice cubes, crushed
1 teaspoon rose water	1 teaspoon rose water
1 tablespoon fresh rose petals	1 tablespoon fresh rose petals

Place the melon flesh in a clean cloth and extract its juice by squeezing, or liquidise. Add the sugar, water, cardamom and ice and whisk. Serve sprinkled with rose water and topped with rose petals for decoration. (For photograph see page 124.)

HOT DRINKS
GARAMA GARAM

In the cold climate of the West, hot drinks like tea and coffee form an integral part of the daily survival kit. Tea has become an international symbol of civilisation and India exports tons of it to the West. The Indians brew a bewildering variety of the drink; a few are given here.

Coffee, on the other hand, is a popular drink too but mainly in the south of India.

Root ginger tea
Adrak ki chaay

This preparation is a panacea for colds and a runny nose.

Preparation time 2 minutes   **Cooking time 10 minutes**   **Serves 6**

METRIC/IMPERIAL	AMERICAN
1 (2.5cm/1-inch) piece fresh ginger root, crushed	1 (1-inch) piece fresh ginger root, crushed
600ml/1 pint water	2½ cups water
1½ tablespoons sugar	2 tablespoons sugar
300ml/½ pint milk	1¼ cups milk

Place the ginger and water in a saucepan and bring to the boil. Cook for 1 minute. Remove from the heat and stir in the sugar and milk. Strain and serve very hot.

Spiced tea

Masaale waali chaay

Preparation time 2 minutes   Cooking time 10 minutes   Serves 4

METRIC/IMPERIAL	AMERICAN
600ml/1 pint water	2½ cups water
2 cloves	2 cloves
1 brown cardamom	1 brown cardamom
4 black peppercorns	4 black peppercorns
1 (2.5cm/1-inch) cinnamon stick	1 (1-inch) cinnamon stick
2 teaspoons tea leaves	2 teaspoons tea leaves
300ml/½ pint milk	1¼ cups milk
1½ tablespoons sugar	2 tablespoons sugar

Place the water, cloves, cardamom, peppercorns and cinnamon in a saucepan and bring to the boil. Stir in the tea and continue to cook over a moderate heat for 2 minutes. Add the milk and sugar and remove from the heat. Strain and serve piping hot. The sugar can be omitted if desired.

Kashmir tea

Kashmiri chaay

Preparation time 2 minutes   Cooking time 30 minutes   Serves 4

METRIC/IMPERIAL	AMERICAN
2 teaspoons green tea	2 teaspoons green tea
300ml/½ pint milk	1¼ cups milk
600ml/1 pint water	2½ cups water
2 tablespoons sugar	3 tablespoons sugar
4 green cardamom pods	4 green cardamom pods
1 (2.5cm/1-inch) cinnamon stick	1 (1-inch) cinnamon stick
1 tablespoon chopped almonds	1 tablespoon chopped almonds

Place all the ingredients in a saucepan. Cover and simmer over a low heat for 30 minutes. Strain and serve scalding hot.

THE CONCLUSION OF A MEAL
HUKKAH, BEEDI AUR PAAN

When everyone has finished eating and the clatter of plates has died down, the gathering then moves to the drawing room. Presently the host wafts in with a tray, carrying the final offering – the paan. The serving of paans to all the guests and the offer of the hukkah or hubble-bubble and *beedis*, Indian cigarettes, to the smokers among them, symbolise the formal conclusion of an Indian meal.

The non-smoking guest usually picks up a paan, puts it in his mouth and, thanking his host, departs. However, in gatherings where there are smokers, there usually follows a session of smoking and paan-eating, after the main meal.

The hukkah or the hubble-bubble has been smoked in Indian homes for centuries and is something of a precursor to the modern smoking pipe. During the Raj, numerous British officers stationed in India regularly rode the palanquins and smoked the hubble-bubble. Many of them maintained the habit after their return to Britain, and even to this day the hukkah is known and smoked in Britain and other places in the West.

Although small and hand-held varieties of the hukkah have always been available, a typical hukkah stands on a pedestal with a conical-shaped metal tank at the base, which is filled with water. Forming the stem between this tank and the conical opening some 1 metre/3 feet up are two pipes. On top of this opening is affixed an earthen chilum – a small bowl with a little spout at the bottom. Some tobacco is placed in the chilum and is covered with burning embers. Sticking out of the stem is a long flexible pipe with mouth-piece at the end. When the chilum has reached the right temperature you inhale from this mouthpiece and it makes a bubbling sound. Hence the name 'hubble bubble' (see page 124 for a drawing of a hukkah).

It is important to remember that the hukkah is an exclusively personal way of smoking and it is usually only available at home. It is smoked by the owner and is offered only to close friends and relatives.

The smokers in the dinner gathering who do not wish to smoke the hukkah normally smoke Indian cigarettes called *beedis*; western style cigars and cigarettes are, of course, smoked, too. Beedis are made from tobacco leaves, by depositing some tobacco powder on them and then rolling them up. The shape of them is broad and round at the top and slightly narrower and flat at the bottom. The shape is then secured by a thread wrapped round it. Beedis come in paper packets and, like cigarettes, range from strong to mild. They are cheap to buy, even by Indian standards.

The paan, served to all guests, is a heart-shaped leaf, almost 10cm/4 inches in length. Paan is made by adding to the leaf first a layer each of edible lime and katechu pastes, then chopped betel nuts and a variety of other ingredients, are heaped on top. The leaf is then folded up into a triangular shape and secured with a clove before being served. On special occasions, paans are served bedecked with edible silver or gold foils, which adds to their already considerable digestive properties.

Paan leaves come in many kinds. There are small luscious green leaves like those grown in the south of India; slightly bitter-tasting and larger leaves from Bengal which, with tobacco, taste perfect to the seasoned paan addict; and the hard, crumbly and pale medium-sized leaves like those grown in Mahoba in Uttar

Pradesh, which seem to be popular all round. As a general guide, paan leaves taste from bitter to sweet. While the professional paan-eaters prefer the bitter variety, the novices who indulge in paan eating for a novelty, are partial to the sweeter type.

Besides the leaves, lime and katechu pastes, several other ingredients are also added in the preparation of paans. Desiccated coconut lends a silky sweet flavour to the paans; betel nuts (*supaadi*), being the main additive, give the paan its 'muscle'. By tradition, betel nuts are chopped with a special cutter called a '*sarauta*' but numerous ready-cut varieties of sweet and scented betel nuts are available in packets. In fact most good Asian shops will have a whole selection of paan ingredients (*paan masala*) to choose from.

Green cardamom is another ingredient commonly used in paans. The Indians eat whole pods of them and also the separated seeds. Another item used in paans is aniseed. It can either be the slim variety, which is eaten as it is, or the 'oversize' type, which is roasted before being served. In some Indian restaurants, roasted aniseeds and Indian sugar candy (*misree*) are the standard offerings when the waiter presents his bill for payment. Cloves are the final ingredient used in a paan, normally applied to secure its folded-up shape. Cloves are also often sucked by themselves to freshen the breath, specially after smoking!

The *paandaan* (an octagonal concave box) is the traditional repository of the paan leaves and accompaniments, and is usually made of brass or silver. The paan leaves are wrapped up in a damp cloth and are placed on the inside tray. This tray is placed over a collection of built-in bowls used for storing the various ingredients and accessories of the paan dish.

The high streets and shopping precincts in India are dotted with small shops, selling paan and cigarettes, rather like the tobacconists one finds in the United Kingdom or the drug stores in the United States. These shops receive continuous swarms of paan-hunters as they come out of the cafés and hotels, cinemas and offices. In Benaras, paan making is something of an art and made-up paans are sold there from as little as a few pence to over £25 each! Benarsi paans are the most famous and are enjoyed by the paan-connoisseurs. The southern Indian variety of paan, on the other hand, is the soft velvety mellow-tasting concoction, favoured by many.

In the Courts of the Mughal Emperors and the Nawabs, paans were served secured with cloves made out of solid gold and silver. These cloves were of course taken out of the paans and thrown away before the paans entered the eager mouths of the royal guests. The maids and other servants were allowed to pick up these cloves and keep them as their tip. These kind of jobs are, alas, no longer available!

The paans round off a meal like nothing else can. Paan leaves and the related ingredients are now freely available in the West. For a photograph of the paan ritual see page 125. So next time you have some guests in for an Indian meal, why not delight them by offering them paans and even your own hubble-bubble?

GLOSSARY OF INGREDIENTS
SAAMIGRIYON KA SHABDKOSH

Aniseed (*patlee saunf*). Used whole or ground. An appetiser and an aromatic, liquorice-flavoured spice; served with paans and for making cordials.

Asafoetida (*heeng*). A strong digestive spice, obtained from a kind of gum resin; has a powerful smell.

Batter drops (*boondi*). Made from gram flour and water into a batter which is then dropped and deep fried in ghee or oil. The little batter drops are then dried and stored in an airtight container and used to make sweets, raitas and curry dishes.

Bay leaf (*tej patta*). An aromatic herb, used fresh or dried for flavouring vegetable and meat dishes.

Bitter gourd (*karela*). An iron-rich green vegetable.

Black beans (*urad dall*). These pulses can be whole or split, with their skin or skinless. Like other dalls they are cooked into a purée. Ground *urad dall* is used in the preparation of many savoury dishes.

Black peppercorns (*kaali/gol mirch*). Said to be the first spice discovered by man; used whole or ground.

Black salt (*kaala namak*). A flavouring agent, used in raitas and other savouries; stronger than plain salt.

Buttermilk (*mattha*). A refreshing, mildly sour liquid obtained by churning skimmed milk; used for making drinks and curried dishes.

Cardamom, brown (*bari illaichi*). A scented spice, used in most vegetable and meat dishes. Larger than green cardamoms.

Cardamom, green (*chhoti illaichi*). Buy in pods or as whole or ground seeds. A fragrant and digestive spice, used in many sweets and savouries; also served with paans.

Carom seeds (*ajwain*). Also known as tymol or omum seeds; used in pickles and vegetable dishes.

Chapaati flour (*roti ka aata*). Sustaining and wholesome starch.

Chilli, green (*hari mirch*). Used fresh or dried. Lends a hot, spicy flavour to food. If preferred, the seeds may be removed before using.

Chilli, red (*laal mirch*). The single hottest spice, used fresh or dried as well as in powder form as cayenne pepper. After preparing fresh chillies wash your hands, and never allow the volatile oils to touch your eyes or face.

Chironji nuts (*chiraunji*). Also known as *charauli*; used in puddings and pullaos.

Cinnamon (*dall chini*). Available in powder or stick form; used in curries, pullaos and sweetmeats.

Cloves (*laung*). These dried flower buds can be bought whole or ground; used in sweets, savouries, spice powders and for pickling.

Coconut (*gari/naariyal*). Used grated, fresh and dried for making sweetmeats and savouries; the milk from its shell is widely used. A commonly used ingredient in southern Indian dishes.

Coriander leaves (*hara dhaniya*). An aromatic herb generally used for flavouring and garnishing.

Coriander seeds (*dhaniya ke beej*). Used whole or ground, they have a light, fragrant, slightly lemony taste and are an essential item in most ground spice mixtures.

Cumin seeds, black (*kaala zeera*). Also known as *shah* (meaning royal) *zeera*. Distinguished from ordinary cumin by its smaller, dark seeds.

Cumin seeds, white (*sufeid zeera*). Used whole or ground; for flavouring and sautéing. An essential ingredient of spice powders.

Curry leaves (*meethi neem*). An aromatic leaf, used green or dry for flavouring.

Dried milk (*khoya*). A milk preparation made from milk powder and water or from boiling creamy milk, used extensively in sweet dishes and some savoury dishes. *Khoya* can also be bought in block form in Asian grocers.

Fennel (*moti saunf*). Buy as vegetable or seeds; aniseed flavoured. Seeds often served roasted, as an after dinner refresher; also used in stuffing and pickles.

Fenugreek leaves (*methi ka saag*). Used for making dry vegetable dishes; rich in vitamin C. A popular leafy vegetable, considered to be a great delicacy in the Punjab.

Fenugreek seeds (*methi ke beej*). Yellow seeds with a strong curry flavour; used in pickles, whole or ground.

Flattened rice (*chewda*). This is made from rice and used a lot in the making of savoury snacks. Available from Asian grocers.

Garam masala (*garam masala*). A mixture of a few hot spices; adds life and flavour to Indian curries and savouries (see page 28). Can be purchased ready-prepared.

Garlic (*lahsun*). A bulb with individual sections called cloves; has a strong pungent flavour.

Ghee (Clarified butter) (*ghee*). An expensive but traditional cooking fat of India; made from butter (see page 13).

Ginger (*taazi adrak*). Buy dried or fresh root, or powdered; fresh is usually grated, after peeling. Adds flavour and has digestive properties.

Gold foil, edible (*sone ka warq*). An edible thin foil used for decorating sweet dishes; aids digestion.

Gram (*bhoora chana*). A very useful grain, rich in protein; gram flour (*besan*) is obtained by roasting and grinding the grams.

Gram flour (*besan*). A binding agent, used extensively for preparing batter.

Green moong beans (dried) (*moong ki dall*). A protein-rich legume, used for making purées and other dall preparations.

Guavas (*amrood*). A delicious fresh fruit, eaten with its seeds; made into chutneys and salads. Can be purchased in cans.

Jaggery (*gur*). Unrefined cane-sugar, also known as molasses; used for making pickles. Being less sweet than sugar, quantities used are larger.

Kewda water (*kewda jal*). A liquid made from the flowers of the kewda plant (pandanus) in the West. Adds fragrance to puddings, cold drinks and rice preparations. Concentrated kewda essence is also available in bottles.

Lady's finger (*bhindi*). *See* Okra

Legumes (*dallen*). Used for making purées and stuffings, an integral part of a vegetarian meal and very rich in protein.

Lime paste, edible (*khaane ka choona*). Used for making the paan dish; also used as a tenderising agent.

Lotus puffs (*makhaana*). When lotus seeds are roasted they puff up and you have makhaanas; used in making puddings and savouries.

Lotus stems (*kamal kakdi*). A cooling vegetable, used in kebabs and cutlets; rich in vitamins and minerals.

Mace (*jaavitri*). The outer membrane of nutmeg, with similar taste; buy as blades or powder. Used in meat dishes.

Mango (*aam*). Used green and ripe; a fruit for making pickles and chutneys as well as sweet dishes.

Mango powder (*aamchoor*). A souring and flavouring agent, made by grinding dried green mango slices.

Melon seeds (*magaz*). Washed and peeled melon seeds are used in many savoury dishes and drinks.

Mint leaves (*podina ki patti*). A herb, used fresh in raitas and chutneys; generally used for garnishing yoghurt-based dishes.

Molasses (*gur*). *See* Jaggery

Mushroom, black (*guchchhi*). A vegetable used for making pullaos and curries.

Mustard oil (*sarson ka tel*). A common cooking oil in southern and eastern India; it has a pungent flavour.

Mustard seeds (*raai*). They can be yellow or black, and are rich in vitamin D and manganese; a souring agent, used for making pickles, sauces and chutneys.

Nigella (*kalaunji*). Black onion seeds, normally used whole. Used for stuffings, pickles, and some meat dishes.

Nutmeg (*jaiphal*). Use whole spice and grate as needed, can be bought ground. Used for flavouring puddings and savouries.

Okra (*bhindi*). A green vegetable, also known as lady's finger; buy when small without any blemishes.

Parsley (*ajmuda ki patti*). A stand-in herb for the green coriander leaves; used for garnishing and flavouring savoury dishes.

Peas (dried) (*sukhi matar*). Dried green peas; used for making chaat dishes and dalls.

Pigeon peas (*arhar/toor dall*). A pulse, the most popular dall ingredient; rich in protein.

Pistachios (*pishte*). An expensive nut, used in puddings, sweetmeats and biriyanis.

Pomegranate seeds (*anaardaana*). Sharp seeds used in making pakodas and samosas, and for flavouring.

Poppy seeds (*khas khas*). A protein-rich aromatic spice.

Preserve, Indian (*murabba*). A specially made variety of the Indian sweetmeat range, which can be stored.

Puffed rice (*layya/murmura*). This is made by dry roasting rice and is used for making both sweet and savoury snacks.

Pulses (*dallen*). Used for making purées and stuffings – and an integral part of a vegetarian meal and very rich in protein.

Pumpkin (*kaddu*). A vegetable cooked in curry or dry form; rich in vitamins.

Radish, white (*mooli*). Indians normally use the white variety of this tangy root; used for making dry vegetables and salads.

Rice flour (*chaawal ka aata*). Obtained by grinding dry or soaked rice; used as a thickening agent, too.

Rose water (*gulaab jal*). An aromatic liquid prepared from fresh roses; used for flavouring sweet dishes; also used for soaking saffron strands.

Saffron (*kesar/jaafraan*). The expensive stigma of the crocus flower, grown in abundance in the Kashmir valley; used for rich yellow colouring and flavouring. Melts quickly in warm water and known as the king of spices.

Sesame seeds (*til ke beej*). Used in making bread and confectionary; serves as a stand-in for almonds. Oil is made from it, too.

Sevs (*sevs*). Vermicelli-like strands, both thick and thin. Made from gram flour.

Silver foil, edible (*chaandi ka warq*). A digestive edible foil, normally used for decorating sweet dishes.

Special gravy (*shorwa/rasa*). Can be made separately, to be used for 'currying up' dry dishes; also served by itself as a sauce.

Sugar candy (*misree*). Served with roasted fennel seeds as a digestive after meals; ultimate form of sugar syrup (see page 19). It is available in packets at Indian grocers.

Sugar syrup (*chaashni*). Made with sugar and water and used extensively in sweet dishes.

Tamarind (*imlee*). A fruit, used in its green and ripe form, for making sauces and chutneys; a souring agent. Tamarind pulp and bottled concentrated tamarind sauce is available at Indian grocers.

Toor dall (*arhar ki dall*). *See* Pigeon peas

Turmeric (*huldi*). Vivid yellow, powdered spice; used for colouring and flavouring; sometimes used as a substitute for saffron.

Vermicelli (*semiyan*). Made into a pudding, from a paste made out of plain flour.

White gourd (*petha*). A vegetable of the pumpkin family, used for making a particular sweetmeat.

Yam (*arbi/ghuiyan*). A starchy vegetable, cooked as curried and dry dishes; also used for making doughs.

INDEX